DATE			

MAJOR VIOLATION

MAJOR VIOLATION

VIOLATION

THE UNBALANCED PRIORITIES IN ATHLETICS AND ACADEMICS

Gary D. Funk, EdD

Leisure Press

Champaign, Illinois

Library of Congress Cataloging-in-Publication Data

Funk, Gary D., 1958-
    Major violation : the unbalanced priorities in athletics and
academics / by Gary D. Funk.
        p. cm.
    Includes bibliographical references and index.
    ISBN 0-88011-441-X
    1. College sports—United States—Moral and ethical aspects.
    2. College sports—United States—Organization and administration.
    3. Athletes—Education—United States.   4. Afro-American athletes-
    -Education.   5. National Collegiate Athletic Association.
    I. Title.
    GV351.F86   1991
    796'.071'173—dc20   90-20653
                                                              CIP

ISBN: 0-88011-441-X

Acquisitions Editor: Brian Holding
Developmental Editor: Holly Gilly
Managing Editor: Dawn Levy
Copyeditor: Jean Tucker
Proofreader: Stefani Day
Production Director: Ernie Noa

Typesetter: Yvonne Winsor
Text Design: Keith Blomberg
Text Layout: Denise Lowry
Cover Design: Jack Davis
Cover Photo: Wilmer Zehr
Printer: Braun-Brumfield, Inc.

Author photo courtesy of Gayle Harper, In-Sight Photography

Printed in the United States of America

10   9   8   7   6   5   4   3   2   1

Leisure Press
A Division of Human Kinetics
  Publishers, Inc.
Box 5076, Champaign, IL 61825-5076
1-800-747-4457

Canada Office:
Human Kinetics Publishers, Inc.
P.O. Box 2503, Windsor, ON N8Y 4S2
1-800-465-7301 (in Canada only)

UK Office:
Human Kinetics Publishers
  (UK) Ltd.
P.O. Box 18
Rawdon, Leeds LS19 6TG
England
(0532) 504211

Photo Credits

For Megan—may she inherit her mother's athletic ability.

Contents

Chapter 6   Solving the Problems, or Creating New Ones?   105

The NCAA and colleges and universities have responded to attacks on their integrity, and the efforts represent the sincere concern of many responsible individuals. Still, as in many other reforms, the mood is too hurried and the goals too shortsighted, and a far too superficial grasp of the problem leaves the involved parties with the reform equivalent of placing Band-Aids on a battleship.

Chapter 7   A Few Sensible Suggestions   133

Various proposals from diverse segments of society have been suggested to improve the college games, and their future implementation could ensure the realization of the wonderful opportunities that intercollegiate athletics can ultimately provide.

Preface

In March of 1989, I was involved in the sponsorship of a literacy awareness program called "Bear Down on Reading." The program featured student-athletes from Southwest Missouri State University (the Bears) who visited elementary schools to emphasize the importance of developing lifetime reading habits. Every visit included a motivational assembly, after which athletes read aloud to students in their own classrooms. The shared books, which had been purchased by local businesses, were donated to the elementary schools' permanent library collections.

A promotional brochure highlighted the goals of the "Bear Down on Reading" program. The front of the brochure featured a photo of a black player from the men's basketball team reading a book to a small white child who sat on his lap. During one of our visits to a local school, a teacher approached me with the brochure and quipped, "I guess we know who teaches the Bears how to read, now." Ha. Ha. Ha.

As academic adviser for the Southwest Missouri State University men's basketball program, I had heard comments like this before, and I shrugged it off while explaining that the player in the picture was a fine student who would graduate at the end of the summer session—which he most certainly did. As the teacher sheepishly walked away, I was again reminded of the old educational adage that students perform up to the expectations people have for them.

There seems to be an implicit message in my encounter with the teacher. It is simply that many people in today's society expect little more from student-athletes than dunks and touchdowns. Oh, sure, there has been much rhetoric over the academic malaise that has spread through intercollegiate athletics. And there has been plenty of finger pointing in the directions of the NCAA, its member institutions, and the student-athletes themselves. Unfortunately, though, much of the concern and related reforms have been superficial, and millions of fans still pay top dollar to enter stadiums and arenas where they can cheer and boo the athletic exploits of young men who are presumably attending an institution to obtain an education.

This societal hypocrisy and the lack of a comprehensive understanding of the academic-athletic issue were the motivating forces behind the writing of this book. I strongly believe no progress will be made in the academic phase of intercollegiate athletics until all parties understand the wide range of factors that affect the situation. *Major Violation* develops this awareness by exploring the academic characteristics of the student-athlete, the universities' treatment of student-athletes, and society's role in the current academic-athletic dilemma. Also, current NCAA "reforms" are reviewed and critiqued. Woven into the examinations of these topics and receiving special attention are the many problems experienced by minority student-athletes in the revenue-producing sports of Division I football and basketball. These two sports have received the most criticism, and it is in these two sports that NCAA institutions have the greatest opportunities to enhance the educational experiences of student-athletes, particularly of those from disadvantaged backgrounds.

Admittedly, much has already been written about academic fraud, recruiting scandals, and financial contradictions in major college athletics. Many writers, though, have chosen to focus on the existing abuses instead of illuminating the underlying problems. While the "symptoms" certainly make for savory reading, constructively dealing with the "disease" is the only way to realize true progress. My goal in this book has been to detail the scope and nature of the underlying problems and to highlight ways to facilitate the realization of the potential opportunities awaiting those who are fortunate enough to participate in intercollegiate athletics. I urge the reader to consider the proposals, and I hope that I have made at least a small contribution to the movement toward ethical intercollegiate athletic competition.

Acknowledgments

I want to thank and recognize Nannette C. Gover for her advice and editorial expertise. Without Nannette's support, this project would not have been possible. Thanks are also due to Royal E. Wohl, who waded through an early draft and made some excellent suggestions. Cathy Crumpley, Joyce Riebe, and Nancy Wilmot provided invaluable help with typing, and Dr. Charles Lippincott ushered me into the age of modern technology.

Very special thanks to Southwest Missouri State University basketball coach, Charlie Spoonhour, and Southwest Missouri State University athletic director, Bill Rowe. Their willingness to honestly examine our own program added greatly to the book and speaks well for their integrity. Finally, I want to thank Holly Gilly and all the kind people at Leisure Press.

1

A Collage

Oklahoma's Will Rogers Turnpike has been the scourge of midwestern motorists for years: They pay $2 a crack for the opportunity to dash 90 miles from the Missouri-Oklahoma state line toward Tulsa through gale-force prairie winds, rampaging truckers, and road signs advertising everything from buffalo ranches to turquoise jewelry. Fall weekends, however—Saturdays in particular—make the drive more endurable. No, spectacular autumn scenery is not an Oklahoma trademark, but any spot on the radio dial will bring you the latest on college football, complete with gridiron-oriented editorials from local talk show hosts and other assorted football crazies. Oklahomans love their football, and the old joke that the Sooner State media covers only two sports, football and football recruiting, gains credence as you meander through airwaves filled with high school scoreboard programs, call-in shows with local experts, and nationally syndicated features highlighting Saturday afternoon's key games. Had you driven through this football frenzy in the fall of 1988, you could have heard the screech of a rock-and-roll guitarist blasting from your radio speaker courtesy of KMOD, Tulsa's progressive rock station—providing yet another, and amazing, rendition of that old Okie favorite, "Boomer Sooner"! You might have been heading to Stillwater to watch Oklahoma State romp Missouri behind the incredible talents of Barry Sanders and Hart Lee Dykes (*Sports Illustrated*'s "Typhoid Mary" of college football recruiting), but you would have been reminded once again of the stranglehold that the Oklahoma University Sooners have on their home state. OSU could recruit 10 Hart Lee Dykes, stomp Nebraska, kick Texas A&M, and play Michigan on the moon, but few Oklahomans would so much as raise an eyebrow as long as OU was pillaging and plundering Longhorn Country during the Battle of the Red River.

A jaunt off the turnpike takes you down state highways and county roads that bisect dusty towns featuring sleepy service stations and brightly colored convenience stores. An inspection of the empty pickups parked here and there reveals the staples of rural Oklahoma life—gun racks, crumpled beer cans, Skoal tins, and faded red OU hats attest to the lifestyles of many who make up the lifeblood of a megaprogram like Oklahoma University's. Whether or not one actually attended Oklahoma University does not matter—allegiance is strong and support unwavering. Nonalumni and nondonors provide massive incentives for the advertisers and media outlets that make the OU football phenomenon possible. Oklahoma has no professional team, and as in Alabama and similar states, the state's pride and ego rest with the fortunes of its collegiate football heroes.

Perpetuating a program at this level requires that Sooner coaching assistants scour the talent-rich regions along the Oklahoma–Texas border for prospective players. Young athletes, often black and often from economically and educationally disadvantaged backgrounds, are thrust into an athletic pressure cooker matched by only a few other major college programs and the 28 professional teams of the National Football League (NFL). They are expected to practice like they have never practiced before. They are expected to conduct themselves in a manner deemed appropriate by the natives. They are expected to make adequate academic progress. They are expected, finally, to WIN!

Some of these expectations are more easily realized than others. For gifted athletes, accomplishments on the playing field may come easily. Common sense can keep a person out of the calaboose. And if an athlete is playing at Oklahoma, he is likely to win. Academics, however, may be an entirely different ball game.

Ron Can't Read, but Who Cares?

"Ron" was a highly sought-after basketball player from the Birmingham area. He could shoot, run the floor, and protect the ball, and his size was excellent. Unfortunately, Ron was a student with undiagnosed learning disabilities who was placed in special education classes to maintain his high school eligibility. During his senior year, Ron received somewhere in the neighborhood of $3,000 to $4,000, an imposter took his ACT for him, and Ron signed a letter of intent with a major southern institution. Ron was a starter for two seasons, but he "flunked out" when a newly hired head coach decided he disliked Ron's attitude.

After 3 years of college Ron's transcript was a sham. Physical education electives, a couple of what had to be bogus history courses (Ron made A's in both), and courses ranging from driver education to football theory composed the bulk of his record. Ron received no diagnostic testing or evaluation and little if any remediation. He was college-caliber, by golly, and providing help would have been an admittance to the contrary. By the end of Ron's academic career, he read at the third-grade level.

What a Story!

Kansas State University has an academic major entitled Social Science, which the college catalog describes as being "sufficiently flexible to allow individual students, in consultation with their advisors, to devise degree programs designed to meet their particular needs, interests, and career goals." One of the electives for this degree is, reportedly, Storytelling for Children. The class explores the history of oral interpretation and how to make stories come to life for the elementary-aged child. The semester highlight is when class members travel to local elementary schools to present stories. One member of one of these biannual trips happened to be a prominent player on the KSU basketball team. The course professor, fearing his student might be unprepared, sent the player to a first-grade classroom, where the audience might be less critical. The professor's suspicions were well founded, as the towering bard had no story ready to tell. Instead, the first-graders were treated to a description of the player's career in the army, with particular attention paid to the social affairs of the barracks. Wide-eyed students and teachers had never heard storytelling quite like this. The course instructor must also have been astounded, as the player received an A for both the project and the class.

What Class Am I In?

Oklahoma State University's architecture program represents one of the stronger academic offerings on the Stillwater campus. Only 60 students are admitted to the program each year, and the numbers usually dwindle during the course of the arduous 5-year program. One School of Architecture academic offering, however, is open to all students enrolled in the university. Introduction to Architecture, which fulfills a university humanities requirement, is a lecture class taught in a large auditorium with audiovisual aids. In contrast to the stringent academic requirements and work standards of the architecture program itself, the approach to Introduction to Architecture is, to say the least, more lax. Students who quickly perceive this laxity flock to the course in hopes of fulfilling general education requirements and garnering easy credit. The resulting large classes hold enrollment figures up, keep departmental budgets healthy, and present an unfortunate professor with the prospect of spending an entire semester with several hundred students who can't distinguish between an arch and a fresco—and couldn't care less. This university's athletic department is a perceptive lot, and many athletes take the class in search of hours and eligibility. Football players are the most predominant and obvious athletic group in the class. Large and often black, the gridders provide sharp contrast to the rest of the mostly white class as they lounge in the back of the auditorium, taking up two or three seats each.

During one past semester, class attendance was terrible, especially among the football players, and those players who were present carried on conversations, fell asleep, even snored loudly. As the semester dragged on, the professor became furious with the situation. He instructed his assistant, a fourth-year female architecture student who helped prepare the class slide shows, to quiet the football players who were conversing and awaken those who were napping. The next lecture found the athletes behaving as usual. With trepidation, the student assistant approached the inattentive, snoring, hulking horde and quietly and politely asked for cooperation. Mildly speaking, she was treated with disdain, and she hurried back to the safety of the slide projector, where she devised a new strategy that the irate professor eventually agreed to implement. Toward the end of each class period, a one-question quiz would be administered to determine attendance and consciousness. The quizzes, worth 10 points apiece, would go a long way toward determining semester grades. The obvious strategy behind the quizzes was to reward those attending and awake and punish those absent or napping.

After each lecture, the student assistant graded the quizzes, and the professor recorded the zeros with a gleeful vengeance. The strategy was mildly effective, as attendance improved. But it soon became apparent that, although their attendance had improved somewhat, the football players were still missing the answers on the quizzes. The professor had not considered the ramifications of failing 20 football players en masse; therefore, he decided to make the questions so simple that they would be impossible to miss. The student assistant, responsible for developing and administering the quizzes, pondered her new instructions and decided to ask the following question: What is the name of this class?

It was a piece of cake, right? It meant 10 easy points for everyone, even the football players. Wrong! The responses included "Engineering," "Art," "History," "Middle Ages," "?," and "I don't know." As the astounded assistant graded the quizzes, it soon became apparent not only that some of the student-athletes failed to pay attention, but also that many hadn't a clue as to what class they were attending.

Check the Books

A certain hoopster whose meandering adventures could best be called nomadic ended up at a St. Louis area community college, where he was immediately enrolled in 12 hours of summer school classes. The player had spent his initial season at a southern basketball power as a redshirt freshman; his second year found him sitting out as a transfer at a well-known midwestern institution where his course record was, at best, ambiguous. Amazingly, though, the sweet-shooting vagabond underwent an academic metamorphosis at the community college and earned 12 hours of A for his summer of toil and study. These achievements greatly pleased the community college's wily and infamous coach, who would have the services of the rejuvenated scholar for the upcoming season.

All was well until the coach discovered that his player's summer schooling constituted what amounted to an excessive number of semesters and, therefore, would disqualify the young man from further junior college competition. The coach, after recovering from the initial shock, began quick and decisive action to rectify the problem. He went to each of the player's instructors and had the A's changed to withdrawals, hoping to eradicate any evidence of the so-called "fifth" semester. Considering the circumstances (four different instructors changing A's to withdrawals did seem unusual), the coach was asked to appear before the junior college eligibility review board. Asked by the chairman of that board to explain how 12 hours of A could have been mistakenly credited and then changed to withdrawals after the fact, the coach bewilderedly shook his head and replied, "Sir, I guess I'd have to call that damn shoddy bookkeeping!"

Victory at Last

Hubert Henderson was an extremely talented basketball player who transferred to Southwest Missouri State University after 3 years at Mississippi State University. Hubert openly admitted that his academic effort at Mississippi State had been less than adequate, and he realized that he would have to improve significantly if he were to remain in good academic standing at his new institution and become eligible for his senior season. I liked Hubert, and I became very involved in his school effort during his year of "sitting out" in accordance with National Collegiate Athletic Association (NCAA) rules. We worked hard on basic skills, and I stressed the necessity for Hubert to assume more responsibility for his own actions.

Hubert's improved attitude and the academic support he received proved successful, and he earned the necessary credits to play the following season—a season anticipated with high expectations for Hubert and the team. As a 6'10" transfer, one who had been third in rebounding and scoring in the Southeastern Conference, Hubert had the locals salivating.

As the eagerly awaited season arrived, it was obvious that Hubert's basketball would flourish. It did, and Hubert drew the attention of professional scouts as his team began to accumulate victories. Hubert's friendly manners and high visibility resulted in many elementary schools and community organizations requesting his presence. While his head coach was noted for encouraging community involvement, Hubert's lack of confidence in his verbal skills prevented him from taking a vital role in community service projects.

Finally, though, Hubert agreed to visit the Good Samaritan Boys' Ranch in a neighboring rural community. It was with trepidation that I drove Hubert out to the ranch, for I had a sneaking suspicion that he would clam up and the entire visit would fizzle.

The arrival of a well-known basketball star was eagerly anticipated by the 30-some boys making up the ranch population. Although the ranch was hardly a detention center, the residents had little interaction with the general public. A visit by someone of Hubert's stature might well be a seasonal highlight. Hubert had hardly arrived before he was surrounded by a group of 14- and 15-year-old boys eager to show off their dormitory, school, barn, and other facilities, especially their new gymnasium. A tall black 22-year-old, Hubert stood out among the short, predominantly white adolescents. But he seemed to gain confidence and display more warmth as the various tours continued, and before long Hubert was seated in a large recreation room with all of the young residents, the staff, and me.

Each kid introduced himself, said how long he had been at the ranch, and told where he came from. Hubert seemed moved at the notion of young teenagers being away from home and family for many months. When the introductions had finished, he stared at the ceiling momentarily, apparently gathering his thoughts or summoning the courage to begin speaking. "Where I grew up, things were pretty tough," said Hubert, and he went on from there. He spoke about parents. He spoke about trust. He spoke about listening. He spoke about responsibility. He spoke about courage. The young audience's attention was riveted, and the staff's eyes were moist. I was stunned, mouth agape. Hubert's talk was moving and inspirational; it was sincere. When Hubert had finished speaking, the entire group, now bonded together, headed to the gymnasium for a demonstration of long-range jumpers and rim-jarring slam dunks. I lingered behind, savoring the moment further. I decided that if Hubert did nothing else during his tenure at the university, what he had done for 30-some troubled kids made the entire experience worthwhile.

The State of Affairs

The state of academics in the Division I athletic environment is sometimes comical, sometimes pitiful, sometimes uplifting, and often saddening. The academic-athletic relationship at major institutions of higher education spans a wide range of educational realities and varying degrees of ethics. The system is scorned by some and questioned by many, and it is under the constant scrutiny of the media, college committees, college administrators, and legislative bodies. It has been pried at, poked at, and peeked at, and the multitude of recommendations to improve it are as far-reaching and diverse as the backgrounds from which the student-athletes emerge. Some parties, such as the Ivy League schools and the band of small liberal arts colleges composing NCAA Division III, would like the Division I beastie to return to the Pandora's box from which it slithered. However, these idealistic opponents of big-time sports should not hold their collective breath, because major college athletics are probably here to stay.

Sports are big business in the United States, and today's "corporate campuses" are microcosms of society at large. Operating from the profit motive, today's universities wage a constant battle for money and resources. Athletics is one of their most marketable products. Alumni may nod favorably and raise an eyebrow over the success of a debate team or a biology graduate student's research project, but the common perception is that nothing will drive the old grads into a frenzied state of donating like a successful and exciting athletic program. Simply stated, athletics is perceived by many to be the quickest and surest method of attracting national media attention and enlisting alumni support for an institution. Admittedly, Harvard, Yale, and other well-endowed universities can effectively and rightfully disagree with this viewpoint; but Eastern Illinois, Memphis State, and Southwest Missouri State cannot—and more than the love of healthy competition keeps Northwestern University in the Big Ten Conference.

The mere existence of this situation does not make it inherently right and proper. In fact, there may be nothing more distasteful than the entire "educators as businessmen" model currently dominating the national educational paradigm. The point is, however, that merely disliking big-time collegiate sports or despising its inherent corruption will not make it disappear. Conversely, accepting Division I athletics for what it is does not mean raising the white flag of surrender. Exploitation and corruption should not be tolerated, and it is the responsibility of educators and concerned constituents to transform athletic programs into a positive facet of the university experience.

Unfortunately, this is not a simple task; passing a single law here or setting a certain standard there cannot address a vastly complex dilemma. Success and progress are attainable, but a thorough examination of the varied and intricate problems associated with the student-athlete is a prerequisite. A problem, remember, always poses a challenge, and a challenge always presents an opportunity.

The problem at face value would appear quite simple. Essentially, the most basic and widely accepted public notion of the student-athlete issue is that institutions of higher education are admitting students who are scholastically inadequate and undeserving of the college opportunity. Though in many instances these suppositions are difficult to deny, acceptance of such a succinct and conclusive belief is a superficial interpretation of a multifaceted situation. To truly understand the problematic nature of major college athletics, we should neither accept nor propose simple direct-line cause-effect relationships and equally simple solutions. A thorough examination of the problems and of their locus in the academic-athletic environment of higher education institutions is needed. Also, the question is not one-dimensional. The deficiencies and needs of the student-athletes, the shortcomings of the institutions themselves, and the structure and pressure of the society that spawns both must be investigated. "If you are not part of the solution, you are part of the problem." Do the present attempts by the NCAA and various institutions constitute pathways to positive growth, or are they merely shortcuts that serve to mask, dilute, and actually aggravate existing conditions? Finally, and maybe most important, the drawbacks and negative aspects of intercollegiate athletic programs must be balanced with the opportunities they present.

The Ultimate Success Story

Kelby Stuckey graduated from a St. Louis inner-city high school in 1985. An unpolished 6'6'' post player, he was lightly recruited. Following old Route 66, Kelby eventually attended Southwest Missouri State University, where he spent his freshman season as a bench-warming cheerleader for an unknown team that, surprisingly, made it to the National Invitation Tourney quarterfinals. His first-year academic progress was adequate, although he was hardly considered a serious contender for the dean's list.

Good things were going to happen to Kelby, though. He had a tremendous work ethic in basketball, and he was always willing to get involved in the community or go talk to a youth group. Kelby Stuckey would become Southwest Missouri State's most popular player: not the best, but certainly the most loved.

Kelby's approach to academics, however, was more lackadaisical than his approach to ball, and I found this personally frustrating. Still, his quick wit and great smile made it hard to stay mad at him, and I will always remember one study hall incident in particular as a prime example of these qualities. I walked into the study lounge to find Kelby sleeping soundly, his head resting on the biology book that he should have been studying for an upcoming test over cell structure and cell reproduction. I nudged him rudely and demanded, "Stuckey, what do you think you're doing?" He looked up slowly and groggily and deadpanned, "Doc, I am learning via osmosis."

Kelby ended up as the starting center for three conference championship and NCAA Tournament teams. He was all-conference 2 years, and, most important, he graduated on schedule with a degree in organizational communications. He went on to play professionally in Germany, where he worked at a community youth center. During the off-season he substitute taught in the St. Louis public schools.

Kelby Stuckey is the ultimate intercollegiate athletics success story. No, he is not making megabucks in the NBA, but he is seeing the world and putting his degree to good use. His tale represents the opportunity that awaits each participant in college sports. Shamefully, it is a scenario replicated all too rarely.

2

The Dumb Jock: Fact or Fiction?

How many Oklahoma University football players does it take to screw in a light bulb?

Only one, but he gets 3 hours of credit for it.

A well-worn joke in Stillwater,
home of Oklahoma State University

Current conceptions of intercollegiate athletics and its participants are varied and often negative. Some view big-time athletics with indignation and disgust. These people see athletic departments as an embarrassment, foulers of pristine ivory tower academic environments. Others express outrage or sadness at the present state of affairs. They perceive the Division I monster as corrupt and exploitative, using disadvantaged young people to achieve an end in which the participants reap little and

11

take even less with them after finishing their athletic eligibility. Another, and quite possibly prevailing, public viewpoint is the tacit acceptance of college athletics as a home for good ol' boys, buffoons, and blacks who are incapable of doing anything more than providing entertainment for thousands of screaming fans. This complacent attitude can probably be found on any campus in the country, and it is a major factor in the media harpooning of all aspects of big-time athletics. Historically, though, except in classical culture, the physical and the intellectual have rarely been perceived as related, and one can only imagine (if lampooning history is permissible) the snickers of Roman patricians as gladiators did battle with wild beasts, Christians, and each other.

American intercollegiate athletics and its players have always been shrouded in clouds of doubt and skepticism. In 1869, the very first year that students from Rutgers and Princeton initiated college football competition, the faculties of the two schools canceled a game because they "feared over-emphasis."[1] And, the turn of the century found the president of the United States lamenting the state of college athletics and the *New York Times* comparing football to the "evils" of lynching (there were 23 football deaths in 1905).[2] Although many of the early concerns with college football focused on excessive violence, questions regarding the relationship of academics and athletics manifested themselves throughout subsequent years.

A 1929 study by the Carnegie Foundation for the Advancement of Education urged that "the recruiting from high school . . . the devotion of an undue proportion of time to training, the devices for putting a desirable athlete, but a weak scholar, across the hurdles of examinations—these ought to stop."[3] Other critics of the era went further, maintaining that colleges were "inculcating incorrect values by emphasizing athletic excellence over academic excellence; contributing to the moral delinquency of students in gambling, drinking, and 'other more or less irreparable orgies.' "[4] These attacks inspired the legendary Knute Rockne, innovative Notre Dame coach and staunch defender of football, to argue that more, not less, football was needed and that youngsters should be given "footballs instead of guns."[5]

Chalk One Up for the Gipper

Unfortunately, even the venerable Rockne was caught in the maelstrom of an intriguing little scandal. It seems that his player George Gipp (of "Win one for the Gipper" fame) was involved in an academic brouhaha that easily could have occurred in the 1990s. Gipp, who lived alone in a South Bend hotel, where he sharpened his skills at cards and pool, was expelled in the spring of 1919 for a variety of academic transgressions. According to Rockne, Gipp was allowed back in school after his performance on an oral examination "amazed" everyone involved. If Rockne's version of the Gipp incident sounds like the hokum passed off on the public by so many of today's coaches, the rest of the story is even more familiar. Father Burns, the Notre Dame president responsible for Gipp's expulsion, was besieged by outraged local citizens, and it was a petition signed by the most prominent of them (not Gipp's oral wizardry) that finally persuaded the good father to readmit the star halfback. Gipp, meanwhile, used his 6-week hiatus from the university to "hustle pool."[6] Although Rockne and the Gipper would come to be immortalized, concern over the academic-athletic relationship continued to mount. By 1934, 41 different studies had been compiled to show that "nonathletes performed slightly better in schoolwork than did athletes."[7]

For anyone remotely familiar with the history of American intercollegiate athletics, these tidbits are hardly revelations. The entire century has seen arguments over the role of big-time college sports, and many one-time powers (the University of Chicago, the Ivy League schools, and several Catholic colleges) eventually chose to deemphasize athletic competition. Still, the Notre Dames and Michigans remain, and they have been joined by a new breed of cat, the Nevada–Las Vegases and the Alabama-Birminghams. The combination of these athletic powerhouses with an explosion of network and cable television coverage has made college athletics more visible and popular than ever.

Abuses in college sports have always existed, but the recent blitz of media exposure has diminished the public's tolerance for academic wrongdoing. America, at least superficially and politically, has decided to demand excellence and accountability in education. The widely distributed and oft-cited A Nation at Risk report (1983) deemed our public education system the equivalent of a foreign invasion and claimed that our illiteracy rate was a threat to national security and technological supremacy. All over the country, state legislatures passed education-oriented bills in a veritable pedagogical frenzy. Exit tests for high school students, standardized teacher eligibility tests, and stiffer entrance requirements for state-supported institutions of higher education became commonplace. Everyone from the president to the local mayor jumped on the educational reform bandwagon, and there were scapegoats aplenty. Naturally, and deservedly, intercollegiate athletics became one of the biggest goats.

Although American society has spent over a hundred years trying to separate the physical from the mental through means as diverse as technology and evangelism, there is a current belief that today's big-time college athlete should be some sort of Astroturf-Renaissance man, spewing forth algorithms as well as play signals. Obviously, such supermen are rare, and the "dumb jock" icon has been a perfect and defenseless target for ridicule and reform. As the sociologist Harry Edwards has stated, "For as long as organized sports participation has been associated with American education, the traditionally somewhat comic, not altogether unappealing "dumb jock" image of the student athlete has endured."[8]

Is this image based on fact, or is it myth perpetuated by a few sensational and widely publicized scandals? Does "Where there's smoke, there's fire" hold true, or has college athletics become just another scapegoat for an educational system under a barrage of attacks? Only a thorough examination of the facts and available information can shed light on these questions, and, even then, formulating a conclusive opinion may be difficult.

Academic Achievement of Student-Athletes

A 1990 NCAA News headline claimed that "Division I athletes are graduating at higher rate than student body." Is this statement factual, or is it merely propaganda? This is not an easy question to answer. Research data on the relationship between athletic participation and academic achievement on the college level has been sporadic at best, conflicting at worst, and difficult to compare because of methodological, population sample, and reportorial differences. The difficulty in assessing college athletes' academic progress is best illustrated by a 1981 study conducted by the American College Testing Program (ACT) for the NCAA, the governing body for the athletic programs of approximately 800 universities and colleges. The ACT investigation attempted to survey 115 colleges and universities that initially agreed to participate in the study. After repeated efforts by ACT, "sufficient data" was gathered from only 46 of the 115 institutions.[9] Nonetheless, the results of the study received recognition, and the findings were used as justification for the NCAA reforms of the mid- to late 1980s.

While the ACT study was often cited, it was at the same time blistered for "serious methodological problems" resulting from the characteristics of the sample, the quality of the data, and inappropriate data analyses.[10] Another study utilized by the NCAA was conducted by Advanced Technology, Inc. in August 1984. This investigation, the "Study of Freshman Eligibility Standards Technical Report," was also criticized for its sample limitations and lack of appropriate analysis.[11]

The intent here is not to lambaste the efforts of ACT or Advanced Technologies, but to shed light on the difficulties of making a clear-cut determination of the academic status of NCAA student-athletes. Even if all 800 universities and colleges responded to a study or survey, the validity of its results would have to be questioned. The primary problem lies in the reporting bias of the respondents. Athletic directors or other university officials might be inclined to report favorably on the academic progress of their student-athletes. This is not to imply that all or any institutions would blatantly fabricate statistics. However, the mere threat of a reporting bias and the difficulty in verifying data for such a widespread study would ensure that any conclusions would be tentative at best.

Obtaining an accurate overall picture of academic progress by student-athletes would require an independent research team visiting campuses selected by a scientific sampling procedure. Obviously, the cost involved in a study of this magnitude would be a major deterrent. Still, although gaining a consensus on the question may not be feasible, several studies highlighting trends and problem areas are worth reviewing. Although these findings are somewhat limited in their application and degree of generalization, their common denominators invite study.

Two areas of academic progress are constantly under discussion in the media, and they are both areas that can be examined quantitatively. Therefore, classroom performance/grade point average (GPA) and graduation rate can be utilized as barometers to determine if the "dumb jock" is a mere media caricature or if serious academic problems exist in intercollegiate athletics.

Classroom Performance

Athletes' grade point averages are discussed and scrutinized as if they represented a consistent and reliable measure of academic progress. COSIDA (College Sports Information Directors of America) Academic All-American team selections are based on them, NCAA postgraduate scholarships are granted because of them, and the nationally broadcast praise of a Keith Jackson or a Brent Musburger reflects their loftiness. Unfortunately, the GPA is a limited measure that, at most, signifies a player's progress in a given program at a given institution. Universal comparison of grade point averages is absurd. Is a Vanderbilt University engineering student with a 2.1 GPA a less able student than a University of Nebraska general studies major with a 3.0 average? Probably not, and this very scenario is why the NCAA has been unable (as of 1990) to pass legislation defining satisfactory progress for eligibility by a graduated grade point average scale ranging from a 1.6 minimum requirement after completion of an initial season to a 2.0 minimum after completion of year 3. (The satisfactory progress issue will be discussed in greater detail in chapter 6.) Still, grade point averages are a favorite topic of discussion, and the old grads with the inside scoops may giggle at Billy Joe's 1.1 GPA or marvel at the fact that a black kid from Chicago can actually make the dean's list.

How do student-athletes compare with "typical" students in terms of GPA and academic progress? While a multitude of applicable data is not available, several studies present some interesting and relevant findings, both positive and negative.

In one widely recognized study conducted from 1970 to 1980 at Colorado State University, the relationship between sports participation and academic progress was observed. The academic progress of all male and female sports participants was tracked and compared with the achievement of nonathletes. While athletes as a whole entered college only slightly less prepared than nonathletes, their actual college performance differed more substantially. University athletes garnered a lower grade point average (2.56 on a 4.00 scale) than did nonathletes (2.74), and the performance gap widened when the variables of race, sex, and individual sport were considered. It seems that black athletes' GPA achievements were significantly lower than white athletes', and that scholarship athletes were less successful than nonscholarship athletes. Although football players logged the lowest grade point average (2.30), the basketball players' average (2.49) included GPAs of female players during 5 years following the introduction of girls' basketball in the mid-1970s. The inclusion of the female players was reported to have inflated the GPA results for that sport. Another clear-cut conclusion from this study was that athletes in revenue-producing sports (football and men's basketball) were the least successful in terms of academic performance.[12]

The Colorado State study poses an intriguing question: Do all athletes perform less successfully than nonathletes, or are academic deficiencies more likely to be shown by certain athletes in specific sports? Findings from this study seemingly imply that, although the athletes' overall grade point average was lower than that of nonathletes, the former may have been influenced by the less successful academic progress of football and men's basketball players. Also, there is an implication that women athletes tend to perform better than their male counterparts. Are these results isolated, or is this a widespread trend?

A 1981 study apparently substantiates the hypothesis that female athletes perform better than male athletes. In fact, this study "found that female athletes' grade point averages were significantly higher than nonathlete students."[13] (The study also reported that athletes' academic achievement as a whole was *not* significantly lower than that of nonathletes.[14]) These results regarding female athletes' academic achievement were reiterated by a 1986 study, "Athletes and Academic Performance: A Study of Athletes at an NCAA Division I Institution." This extensive investigation categorized student-athletes "by sex, grant-in-aid status, race, and as participating in either a revenue (football and men's basketball) or non-revenue sport."[15] Female athletes, according to the study, achieved significantly higher grade point averages than male athletes participating in both revenue and nonrevenue sports (see Table 2.1).

Like the Colorado State study, this Division I study shows female athletes outperforming all students, and male athletes in the revenue sports

Table 2.1   Selected Grade Averages for Sex-Revenue Combinations

Athlete category	Total grade point average
Female athletes	2.87
Male nonrevenue athletes	2.47
Male revenue athletes	2.25
Overall university	2.57

Source: Ann M. Mayo, "Athletes and Academic Performance: A Study of Athletes at an NCAA Division I Institution," *Academic Athletic Journal*, Fall 1986, 27.

of football and basketball lagging behind. These findings were further reiterated by the 1987–88 National Study of Intercollegiate Athletics that found women basketball players earning significantly higher GPAs than men did—an average of 2.640 to 2.440.

A further inspection of the Division I study reveals more illuminating data when athletes' progress is broken down according to grant-in-aid status and race (see Table 2.2).

This table points out two glaring statistical differences. First, full-grant athletes scored significantly lower than partial-grant or no-grant athletes. Second, again in congruence with the findings of the Colorado State study, GPAs of black male revenue sport athletes were significantly lower than those of white male athletes. Obviously, the majority of full

Table 2.2   Grade Averages by Grant-in-Aid Status and Race

Athlete category	Total grade point average
Grant-in-aid status[a]	
Full grant	2.44
Partial grant	2.71
No grant	2.64
Overall university	2.54
Race[b]	
White male revenue	2.51
Black male revenue	1.99

[a]Ann M. Mayo, "Athletes and Academic Performance: A Study of Athletes at an NCAA Division I Institution," *Academic Athletic Journal*, Fall 1986, 28.
[b]Ibid., 30.

grants (full-ride scholarships) usually are awarded in the revenue sports of football and men's basketball, where in the Division I study 41 percent of the participants were black, compared with 5 percent in the nonrevenue sports. Equally disturbing in regard to the minority issue is the academic performance of blacks in basic education requirement classes. While the average black athlete GPA was 1.99, in basic education requirement classes ("core required classes in the areas of mathematics, humanities, sciences, and social sciences"[16]) the average GPA for black male revenue sport athletes plunged to 1.77. This was particularly disturbing to the investigators because a formula using students' high school rank and ACT composite scores had predicted an average GPA of 2.11 for black males participating in revenue sports. The discrepancy between the black males' predicted and actual grade point averages contradicted the findings for female athletes, who overachieved (2.87 total grade point average compared to a predicted 2.75) and for white male revenue sport athletes, who also performed better than anticipated (2.51 total grade point average compared to 2.44 predicted). The achievement gap for black athletes is most distressing because the difference between the basic education requirement GPA (1.77) and the predicted figure (2.11) may be "the best measure of whether a student is attaining his potential."[17] Unfortunately, a 1977-to-1983 study of University of Michigan scholarship football players also found blacks (2.12 grade point average) achieving less than nonblacks (2.44 grade point average).[18] And a 1988, $1.7 million NCAA study conducted by American Institutes for Research (AIR) found that cumulative grade point averages for football and basketball players (2.46) were lower than the average GPAs of players in other collegiate sports (2.61).[19] The NCAA study also reported that black football and basketball players had a cumulative GPA of 2.16 at predominantly white institutions and 2.21 at predominantly black institutions. This compared unfavorably to the 2.48 cumulative GPA for nonblack football and basketball players.[20] Other studies have produced similar findings.[21]

If grade point averages are the sole indicator of academic progress, a problem certainly exists. Athletes in the revenue-producing sports of football and men's basketball apparently perform less successfully academically than female athletes, athletes in nonrevenue sports, and "typical" students making up the overall student body. This unfortunate circumstance is most noteworthy considering the integral, if not primary, roles that black athletes have assumed in Division I football and basketball during the last 2 decades. A glimpse at any NCAA Division I Final Four reveals the prevalence of black players. At the 1990 Final Four, for instance, 37 of the 55 players representing UNLV, Duke, Arkansas, and Georgia Tech were black. Unfortunately, many of these black players may be experiencing the most academic difficulty.

Graduation Rates

Fortunately, the GPA is not the sole determinant of academic success, and thanks to the Privacy Act, a player—unless he or she is an outstanding scholar—is usually and mercifully spared from having his or her grade point average plastered over the print pages or bandied about the airwaves. Although there have been exceptions, graduation rates have usually received the most publicity as a symbol of an athletic program's academic success. Memphis State, for example, had its reputation sullied by published reports that the university graduated only 6 of 58 basketball players between 1977 and 1983.[22] Adding to the embarrassment was the fact that all 6 were white—at a school that has traditionally had many black players. On the opposite end of the spectrum is Duke, a school that, according to reports, graduates 100 percent of its basketball players and is constantly glorified for its academic achievements. However, like grade point averages, graduation rates have some real shortcomings as a measuring stick for a program's academic integrity.

Statistical analysis in itself can be corruptible and misleading; it is erroneous to assume that one school's 25 percent graduation rate for athletes is automatically comparable to another school's 75 percent rate. Here is an example. Assume that School A (25 percent graduation rate) and School B (75 percent) have comparable athletic programs including base-

Table 2.3 Data for Graduation Rates at Hypothetical Schools

| | School | |
Athlete category	A	B
Athletes initially enrolled (1985)	100	100
Athletes who transferred	10	10
Athletes who quit teams and school	35	40
Athletes who quit teams but stayed and graduated in 1989	5	5
Athletes who used up athletic eligibility and dropped out of school	5	4
Athletes who used up eligibility but are still matriculating	20	34
Athletes who graduated in 1989	25	7

School A claims its graduation rate is 25% (25 / 100 = 25%).
School B claims its graduation rate is 75% (12 / 16 = 75%).

ball, basketball, football, and track and field, and that their publicly announced graduation rates reflect the class of 1989, which enrolled in 1985. For the sake of simple mathematics, assume that both schools recruited 100 athletes garnering the academic results shown in Table 2.3.

School B, obviously, has formulated a creative equation. School A maintains that 100 athletes were recruited and 25 of the recruited athletes graduated, as simple as that. School B, however, has chosen not to include transfers, athletes who quit, and athletes who are staying in school in an attempt to complete degree programs. School B also includes students who quit athletics but remained in school and graduated, whereas even these students are excluded from School A's graduation rate formula. School B's mathematical rationale is that the school had no control over students who transferred or quit, and that athletes continuing their scholarly endeavors should not be included in the calculation until their fate is determined. Admittedly, School B makes a valid, albeit convenient, point.

Neither School A nor School B has contrived a formula that is wrong or unethical. They are, however, both using incorrect graduation rate formulas according to the *NCAA Manual*. Bylaw 5-6-(e)-(4), which requires a Division I institution's chief executive officer to provide annual graduation rate information, states:

> GRADUATION RATES. The report shall include the institution's graduation rate for the entering freshman class that began attendance as full-time, regularly matriculated, degree-seeking students at the institution six years prior to the regular fall term that includes the October 1 deadline established in 30.1, for both recruited student-athletes and students generally. For purposes of this legislation, the "graduation rate" shall be based upon the number of students who entered the member institution with no previous collegiate attendance and graduated from that institution within five academic years of the date of initial enrollment.

> ADJUSTED GRADUATION RATE. The report shall include the institution's adjusted graduation rate for recruited student-athletes in each sport. In calculating the adjusted graduation rate, transfer student-athletes shall be included as a part of the class that had completed degree credit equivalent to the degree credit completed by the transfer student-athletes and accepted by the certifying institution at the time of transfer. A student-athlete who left the institution while in good academic standing and who would have met the satisfactory-progress requirements for athletics eligibility if the student-athlete had returned for the following academic term shall not be included. Student-athletes who did not graduate within the specified five-year pe-

riod but who continue to be enrolled as full-time students at the same institution and maintain satisfactory progress toward a specific baccalaureate degree also shall not be included.[23]

One can only imagine athletic directors and coaches muddling through that bit of mumbo jumbo, and it is no wonder that graduation rates have a certain air of unreliability about them. Even if Bylaw 5-6-(e)-(4) were followed to the letter, there is nothing to prevent institutions from using an entirely different formula in presenting graduation rates to the media and the public.

Another major problem with comparing institutions' graduation rates is that even if statistical and reporting methods could be standardized, the comparison of these rates might yield little relevant information. As with grade point averages, comparing graduation rates from school to school is like matching apples and oranges. Though a university reporting a 10 percent graduation rate for its athletes should, at the very least, come under scrutiny, an institution flaunting a 100 percent graduation rate might warrant equal suspicion. This is not to say that an immediate investigation of Duke and its reported success should be forthcoming. Duke, Notre Dame, and other prestigious schools have excellent athletic traditions and can maintain high standards and admit quality athletes who are academically capable.[24] However, some situations are peculiarly fishy, and varying degrees of informational latitude may be displayed by individual institutions of higher education. Thus, accurate comparisons of graduation rates may not be feasible or equitable, and comparing institutions with stringent standards to those whose primary requirement is the "feather test" is inherently unjust. (With the feather test, a person who can discernibly blow a feather is admitted; if 4 years later the person can still demonstrate this feat, a diploma is awarded.)

Despite the discrepancies and inequities, graduation rates remain a prominent topic of discussion. Their perceived utility as a measure of academic integrity is such that two pieces of proposed federal legislation have included graduation rates as a litmus test for an institution's academic propriety.

Legislating Graduation

In 1985, U.S. Representative James J. Howard (Democrat, New Jersey) proposed a bill (H.R. 2620) that would require colleges and universities to graduate "at least 75% of their scholarship athletes within five years in order for contributions to their athletic departments to qualify as tax deductible."[25] Although Representative Howard's bill failed to become law, as of July 1990 another piece of legislation is awaiting approval from the House of Representatives. Sponsored by two congressional representatives who are former professional basketball players, Tom McMillen (Democrat, Maryland) and Ed Towns (Democrat, New York), the "Student Right-to-Know and Campus Security Act" (H.R. 1454) would require colleges and universities receiving federal funds to "report annually the graduation rates of students with athletic scholarships, and how long it took them compared to all students." The Senate has already passed a graduation rate disclosure bill, and the two bills must be reconciled before they can be sent to the president's desk. Senator Bill Bradley (Democrat, New Jersey), who sponsored the Senate bill, explained that the motivation for the legislative action was the "single-minded devotion to athletics among our nation's schools and colleges," and he added that this "can lead to exploitation and abuse of our young athletes."[26]

These are lofty words indeed. If graduation rates are to be so scrutinized and effectual in the future, reviewing what knowledge exists about them would be beneficial.

Ascertaining a conclusive national graduation rate for student-athletes is virtually impossible. The hindrances affecting grade point average research and the two previously discussed problems concerning graduation data seriously hamper any efforts to determine credible figures. However, several studies provide a partial glimpse of the graduation rate picture, and individual horror stories and isolated tales of documented neglect abound in today's media and can be located in the libraries' dusty periodical archives (see box on p. 23).

These lamentable happenings should not necessarily be viewed as indictments of the institutions mentioned. In fact, some of these schools should be applauded for admitting what other colleges will not. Although most of these institutions have initiated reform during the past decade, graphic examples of academic neglect continue to be a source of embarrassment for intercollegiate athletics and for institutions that are otherwise highly regarded. Do these examples of poor graduation rates indicate a widespread national problem, or is this yet another case of the dirtiest laundry surfacing in a sensational manner? Answering this question with any degree of certainty is difficult because "few empirical studies exist" that examine the relationship between student-athletes and their academic achievement, particularly in terms of graduation rates.[27] Still, the few existing studies shed some light on the scope of the graduation problems.

The Party Line

The NCAA contends that its consistent finding has been "that the graduation rate for student-athletes has been higher than that of the student body." To support this contention the NCAA cites its 1989 Division I Academic Reporting Compilation (see Table 2.4), a comprehensive yet generic overview of student-athlete graduation rates. Graduation rates

Graduation Rate Horror Stories

- An early 1973 study found that University of Tennessee athletes had more problems than typical students fulfilling graduation requirements because of the amount of time required for sports participation.[a]
- At the University of Texas at Austin, only 39 percent of basketball players *entering* the school between 1975 and 1981 obtained their degrees, whereas 54 percent of the student body as a whole obtained degrees.[b]
- At North Carolina State University, in the classes of 1976, 1977, and 1978, only "two of 80 entering football players graduated. None of the 15 basketball players in those classes earned degrees."[c] According to some reports, the situation in Raleigh improved little during the years Jim Valvano was the head basketball coach.
- More than 200 blacks have played on University of Georgia athletic teams, "but as few as 15 of these athletes may have actually graduated."[d]
- The University of the District of Columbia can only estimate the graduation rate for athletes during the 10 years from 1977 to 1988. James McIver, vice president for student services, says that between 12 and 16 athletes graduated out of literally hundreds who participated in football, basketball, tennis, and track.[e]
- In 1989 a conference-wide survey of the Big 8 showed that only 9.3 percent of black seniors who played basketball and football during the 1989 season actually graduated.

Note. [a]Robert J. Ballantine, "What Research Says: About the Correlation Between Athletic Participation and Academic Achievement." ED233994, 1981, 4. [b]Alvin P. Sanoff and Kathryn Johnson, "College Sports' Real Scandal," *U.S. News and World Report*, 15 September 1986, 62. [c] Jerome Cramer, "Winning or Learning? Athletics and Academics in America," *Phi Delta Kappan*, May 1986, K-3. [d] Ibid., K-2. [e] Susan Oberlander, "New Athletic Director at U. of District of Columbia Will Try to Rescue a Floundering Program," *The Chronicle of Higher Education*, 2 November 1988, A33-A34.

for 11 men's sports and 10 women's sports (track and cross country considered two sports) are detailed, along with a combined rate for 7 minor men's sports and a combined rate for 4 minor women's sports. In every comparable sport, women did as well as or better than men, and no female sport had a median graduation rate lower than 50 percent. Among males, on the other hand, the report shows 4 different sports' median graduation rates below the 50 percent level, with the revenue-producing sports of football (37.5 percent) and basketball (33.3 percent) settling at rock bottom.[28]

Unfortunately, the NCAA compilation provides no information on the success of minority student-athletes, nor is it possible to compare the student-athlete graduation rates with those of each institution's general student body. Still, reviewing ACT data on national graduation rates does allow for some comparison between the success of student-athletes and their nonathletic peers (see Tables 2.4 and 2.5).

Any conclusions from the comparisons of two methodologically different studies should be drawn with caution, however.

Other studies offer more specific, albeit more isolated, data. The aforementioned Colorado State study found that athletes had a lower graduation rate (34 percent) than did the general CSU student population (44.8 percent). Again, as with grade point averages, football players were the least successful group in the sample, with a graduation rate of 26.8 percent.[29]

Some research apparently contradicts specific aspects of the Colorado State study findings, however. A study of University of Michigan football players published in 1987 reported that 65.9 percent of the players graduated during a 6-year period under study.[30] While the Michigan figure appears significantly higher than the graduation rate figure for Colorado State athletes, these figures may reflect only the differences between two diverse programs studied at different times. Other studies, however, also seem to negate the Colorado State overall data. Both the ACT and Advanced Technology studies, previously noted as having been criticized for methodological shortcomings, concluded that male athletes graduated at a rate about equal to or higher than that of male nonathletes or students in general.

Although arriving at a conclusion may be presumptuous, it would appear that athletes in general graduate at a rate near or above the 40 to 48 percent national figure. The status of male minority student-athletes is less clear, however, and few definitive studies are available that specifically address minority athletes' graduation figures. While many tangible examples (Georgia, Memphis State, University of the District of Columbia, etc.) seem to point to minority graduation rates as problematic, widespread quantitative data is sparse. Two statistical examples, however, apparently support the consensus portrayed by the media. The Michigan study and its findings on graduation rates mirror the problem experienced by minority student-athletes in the area of grade point averages. Although 65.9 percent of all athletes surveyed in the study graduated, only 52.7 percent of blacks received degrees. The black student-athlete rate pales further when compared to the nonblack graduation rate of 74.4 percent.

Table 2.4 Graduation Rates by Sport

	All-male or mixed teams			All-female teams	
Sport	Number of schools in study	Median graduation rate (%)[a]	Sport	Number of schools in study	Median graduation rate (%)[a]
Baseball	238	50.0	Basketball	263	60.0
Basketball	270	33.3	Field hockey	71	80.0
Football	194	37.5	Golf	67	66.7
Golf	179	50.0	Gymnastics	77	66.7
Gymnastics	37	50.0	Softball	141	66.7
Soccer	160	66.7	Swimming	140	75.0
Swimming	145	60.0	Tennis	190	75.0
Tennis	202	66.7	Track/cross country	179	57.1
Track/cross country	227	47.6	Volleyball	202	66.7
Wrestling	108	50.0	All others (4 sports)		100.0
All others (7 sports)		80.0			

$$^{a}\text{Graduation rate} = \frac{\text{Number of students who graduated by 1988}}{\text{Number of students who entered in 1983}} \times 100$$

Source: *The NCAA News*, 13 June 1990, 12.

Table 2.5   National Graduation Rates by Level of Selectivity

Selectivity[a]	Graduation rate (%)	
	Public university	Private university
Highly selective	61.4	82.0
Selective	54.8	66.4
Traditional	52.4	55.6
Liberal	45.4	48.7
Open	40.7	42.5

[a]Self-reported

Southwest Missouri State University is another example of the discrepancy between the graduation rates of black and white student-athletes. SMSU, a comprehensive regional institution with an enrollment of more than 20,000, has flirted with national success in basketball by appearing in the NCAA Division I postseason tourney for four consecutive seasons. With an overall graduation rate of 46 percent (utilizing the NCAA formula as outlined in Bylaw 5-6-(e)-(4)) from the years 1982 to 1990, the basketball program's graduation rate was higher than the national median graduation rate for Division I basketball programs (33 percent) and even bettered the overall SMSU graduation rate of 38 percent. Despite this relevant success, a closer examination of the situation reveals a serious problem. Although the 46 percent team graduation rate may or may not be noteworthy, the glaring difference between the white graduation rate of 93 percent and the black graduation rate of 35 percent *is*. The SMSU figures are supported by the 1989 Big 8 Survey, in which the black graduation figure of 9.3 percent compared unfavorably with the white graduation rate of 48.9 percent. This unfortunate contrast is a national trend. When one considers that 52 percent of Division I basketball players and 36 percent of Division I football players are black, the ramifications are staggering.[31]

The Bottom Line

Is the "dumb jock" image a myth? Possibly. Does big-time intercollegiate athletics as a whole deserve the criticism it has been forced to endure? Maybe not. Although these questions are answered somewhat cautiously, there is enough evidence to conclude that student-athletes in general are performing satisfactorily in the classroom. In fact, some segments of the student-athlete population outperform their nonathlete counterparts. Many NCAA sports (see Table 2.4) record outstanding graduation rates, and woman athletes in particular seem to enjoy tremendous success in both the GPA and graduation rate categories. Several theories have been postulated to explain the academic success realized by those young people who are student-athletes in the true sense of the term. Association with achievement-oriented peers, transference of achievement values from sports to the classroom, an increase in self-esteem that creates a higher level of aspiration in other domains, internal and external pressure, and more scholastic and career guidance from significant adults have all been cited as reasons why student-athletes may do as well as or better than typical students.[32] Woman athletes, according to a Texas Tech University researcher, even have a higher degree of moral development. Although moral reasoning abilities do not necessarily correlate with academic performance, women's athletic programs have realized excellent academic success.[33] There is too much quantitative evidence to deny that female student-athletes perform very well in their scholastic endeavors. However, I sincerely doubt that either innate womanhood or superior moral reasoning has anything to do with it. This topic will be dealt with in chapter 4.

If the overall student-athlete population performs adequately, and if female student-athletes achieve exceedingly well, then what is causing all the ruckus?

Unfortunately, the public at large just does not care about men's tennis or women's field hockey. Whether it is right or wrong, the majority of the sports associated with outstanding graduation rates simply do not command the attention of the media or the sports-loving public. Certainly each has its own sphere of ardent support, but these nonrevenue sports are just that. Their existence at many Division I institutions is attributed solely to the NCAA requirement that Division I ("major college") institutions "sponsor a minimum of eight varsity intercollegiate sports." Thus, as the remarkable win-loss record of State U's women's volleyball team goes unnoticed, so might the squad's outstanding academic accomplishments. As unreasonable and discriminatory as this may seem, these are, to quote Porter Waggoner, "the cold, hard facts of life."

Football and basketball—men's basketball—are what people care about, and these are the two traditional revenue-producing sports. Some women's programs (i.e., basketball at the University of Tennessee) have become popular, but football and men's basketball are what draw national media attention and generate millions of dollars. These scenarios, however, are predicated on winning, which requires an abundance of extraordinary athletic talent. A large pool of this extraordinary ability can be found in the poor black neighborhoods of inner cities and the equally poor rural regions of the South.

The Cold, Hard Facts

Bluntly put, academic abuses and problems are most prevalent in the two high-profile revenue-producing sports, and often these problems involve black or minority student-athletes. The problems of educationally disadvantaged black athletes are clear to anyone who has ever seriously studied the high-revenue sports and their relationships to academics. The statistical data does nothing to refute these impressions. The headline cases are troublesome proof of the academic problems surrounding black players. Memphis State University, whose problems have already been detailed, has for years featured a predominantly black basketball team. The University of Georgia fiasco specifically highlighted the academic neglect of black athletes, and there are many other highly publicized educational heresies.

Scandals

Creighton's Kevin Ross, UCLA's Billy Don Jackson, and North Carolina State's Chris Washburn were all involved in "scandals" that received a great amount of media attention. Ross sued his former institution (Creighton) for passing him along academically when he could not read; Jackson, another nonreader, died of a drug overdose; and Washburn's alleged involvement with theft, gambling, and bogus course work was partially responsible for the dismissal of his highly successful coach, Jim Valvano. Interestingly, all of these players are black.[a]

Note. [a]Jerome Cramer, "Winning or Learning? Athletics and Academics in America," *Phi Delta Kappan*, May 1986, K-4.

The widespread media attention given to incidents such as these is obviously due in good part to the extreme visibility of the two sports themselves. There is, however, another factor. Though the United States may be one of the planet's more pluralistic nations, there is nonetheless a clear-cut white majority. This white majority is even more evident when the demographics of college graduates and professionals—the financial and working lifeblood of universities and colleges—are considered. Thrust into predominantly white environments are scholastically unprepared blacks from predominantly black communities. It is no wonder that their trials and tribulations are so conspicuous. Freelance writer Jerome Cramer wrote of a conversation with a Washington, DC, sportswriter who stated, "Once the athlete stopped being somebody's tall farm kid from downstate and instead became a strange, big (and increasingly black), dumb kid from the ghetto who no one cared about, then it became clear the athlete really was an outsider."[34] One can only imagine the consequences if George Gipp had been black. And the old rockabilly song may have been most prophetic when it proclaimed in reference to a common crime, "If I'd been a black man, they'd a given me thirty years."

Proclaiming that intercollegiate athletics' academic problems primarily surface in the revenue sports of football and men's basketball and that black student-athletes are often the foci of these problems is not sufficient. This simple statement offers no solutions, and it streamlines an issue laden with complexities and contradictions. Although the student-athlete dilemma may often be "black," many nonblacks are struggling too. More often than not, they may have problems for the same reasons as their black teammates. Unfortunately, grappling with problems steeped in complexity and contradiction is neither easy nor pleasant, and the modern tendency (the NCAA tendency as well) is to plan and implement a short-term and inflexible solution and hope for the best. Quick-fix approaches will not work here, though, and a comprehensive and thorough examination of the student-athletes, the institutions they attend, and the larger society is necessary before any meaningful solutions can be implemented.

3

The Roles and Educational Characteristics of the Student-Athlete

Home means security, and so does the high school sweetheart whose junior year involves cheerleading, Typing II, and skepticism over "going all the way." Home is also a place usually free of unpleasant surprises, with plenty of coaches, relatives, and well-wishers to prevent adolescent temptations from leading one totally astray and to quickly rectify matters if they do. Finally, home is the small pond well-stocked with adulation. College, however, disrupts and sometimes mines this safe and familiar path. Mom no longer cooks breakfast, Mary Sue is unavailable for fraudulent homework assistance, and the days of being the first-look option in the hastily drawn game-winning play diagram may be gone forever. It is a wonder that more freshman student-athletes—no longer enjoying stardom, and facing a rigorous schedule of practices and class assignments—do not pack up and head down the nearest "lost highway" to home sweet home.

Adjusting to Changing Environments

Conjecture and melodrama aside, student-athletes do encounter many changes as they begin their college careers. These problems, however, are not exclusively theirs, and the sometimes traumatic transitions facing student-athletes are shared by their nonathlete cohorts. All beginning students face major adjustments, and the increased needs for academic preparation, emotional and physical stability, and proper time management can sometimes be overwhelming.

Academic preparation is often very difficult for first-time college students. Becoming familiar with college resources can be task enough, and attempting to assess and refine skills and learning styles in a challenging and pressurized academic environment can compound already existing tensions. Independent learning, or accepting responsibility for one's education, is another challenge facing many freshmen. Too often elementary schools, middle schools, and senior high schools offer their students few opportunities to initiate or participate in personal educational goals and strategies. The cattle-herding approach all too prevalent in public education does little to provide students with experiences that prepare them for the wide variety of academic decisions they will have to make.[1]

Beginning college can also mean an increase in stress and tension, often resulting from both external and internal pressures. Grades and the academic expectations of family and peers are external strains that can wear down the healthiest of young minds and bodies, and the internalized pressures related to social acceptance can erode in an even more damaging manner. Aspiring to soar to mythical heights, students all too often fall prey to the "broken record syndrome," allowing themselves to get bogged down in a mental rut by reliving past failures and punishing themselves with notions of what they should have done.[2] Eventually these stresses take their physical and mental toll, and many students never do learn to cope successfully.

Time management and organization demands, more than any other factors, may also lead to the demise of many well-intentioned students.

New college students often lack the structural skills that are necessary to manage studies and time more effectively. A report published by the United States Department of Education "revealed that 68 percent of high school seniors spend fewer than 5 hours per week on homework. More than 70 percent of all seniors revealed that poor study habits interfered with their education."[3] Time management and study habits can be learned, but balancing social activities with academic priorities is a problem some students never conquer.

While all college neophytes face hurdles, not *all* student-athletes enter college at a distinct academic disadvantage. In fact, four studies conducted between 1967 and 1977 found not only that athletes attained higher high school grade point averages, but that their "educational aspirations, self-concepts, and other effective characteristics were enhanced by (athletic) participation."[4] The findings of a 1989 "Minorities in Sports" study conducted by the Women's Sport Foundation support these earlier studies. Tracking 14,000 students for 6 years, the study found that minority varsity athletes achieved higher grade point averages than minority nonathletes. The report went on to state that sports held many young people in school, and that minority athletes were more "socially involved" than minority nonathletes.

Obviously, though, very few high school athletes continue their athletic careers at the Division I level, and to generalize the findings from the 1989 Women's Foundation study and the earlier investigations would be nothing short of ludicrous. Many beginning Division I athletes are plagued with serious academic deficiencies, and they are faced with other obstacles peculiar to their student-athlete status. Even the "Minorities in Sports" study admitted that athletic success in high school does not ensure upward mobility after the secondary years.

The Plight of the Student-Athlete

A student-athlete's reason for attending an institution of higher education may be problematic in itself. School is often viewed as the avenue to athletic exploits rather than vice versa, and the very nature of a student-athlete's attendance at a college or university may prevent academics from becoming a top priority.

The Athletic/Academic Quandary

The athletic scholarship is partially responsible for this situation. Whether or not an athletic scholarship recipient is a conscientious student, the undeniable reality is that the young person is attending a particular institution to participate in a given sport. This fact is reinforced each waking moment by the media, fellow students, and the ever-present coaches themselves. All student-athletes must face the prima facie negative prioritization of academics, and even the finest academic institution might say *adios* to a hoopster who would quit the team but ask to keep his scholarship in order to pursue his newfound interest in archaeology.

Self-Responsibility

Another problem inherent in collegiate athletics is the student-athlete's stunted development of responsibility. While the absence of Mom's cooking and Mary Sue's assistance may be an initial shock, there are nonetheless many people quite eager to help a talented young athlete on his way. Specialized coaches build strength and skills, academic advisers and tutors freely give advice and help, and charitable boosters are always available to provide special amenities. This special status gives a sense of false security because in the long run, academic and vocational success depend on a young person's ability to take responsibility for himself. Of course, there are always exceptions. Some institutions award degrees as generously as boosters give new sweaters at Christmas, and the Michael Jordans of the world (or of the galaxy, as in Jordan's case) will always be able to ply their trades quite admirably. Mere mortals attending institutions where they must earn a degree will, however, eventually have to realize that the silver platter mysteriously vanishes with the last arcing jump shot or the final gut-busting touchdown. (Michael Jordan, by the way, graduated in 1985, from the University of North Carolina with a BA in geography.)

Derecruitment

Perhaps one of the greatest initial shocks to the student-athlete is the process of "derecruitment." Every first-time student confronts doubts and possible trauma, but the "breaking down" of glorified athletes within their athletic realms has a debilitating, pervasive effect on many freshmen. The courtship of scholastic athletes by major colleges is one of the more grossly inane adventures occurring in today's society. Athletic programs spend thousands of dollars on their efforts to persuade 17-year-olds to become Bears, Tigers, or Horned Frogs. Prospective student-athletes and their families are besieged by fast-talking coaches, and the saccharine efforts of middle-aged men inflate egos and sometimes pocketbooks. The case of Stacy King, former Oklahoma University All-American center, is a perfect example of the level of absurdity that even "legal" recruiting escapades can reach. King, an outstanding prospect from Lawton, Oklahoma, had intimated to members of the media that he would sign with Oklahoma State University and then-coach Paul Hansen. On a Friday before the national signing date, however, a black limousine picked King up in front of his high school, and the all-state performer was not seen for the entire weekend. When King returned from his mysterious journey, he announced his revised intentions of signing with Billy Tubbs and his Oklahoma University Sooners. Extraordinarily enough, the entire fantastic episode was covered by the Oklahoma media and, presumably, did not raise the eyebrows of NCAA enforcement officers. Still, the dramatic event illustrates the extent to which coaches and programs will go to ingratiate themselves with players and their families.

Inflated egos and promises of stardom are fine for a while, but any coach worth his salt understands that 30 prima donnas strutting around a football practice field can make a mentor's life somewhat miserable. So, with the hot August sun beating down on preseason practices, coaches begin to cut down their egotistical novices one notch at a time. Going from a future All-American to a "worthless piece of shit who will never play a goddamn minute" could be tough for anyone, but for an 18-year-old it can be utterly frightening. There is no doubt that "derecruitment"—described by a former University of Missouri assistant football coach as the toughest part of the job—adds stress to an already stressful time.

Becoming a Small Fish in a Big Pond

Adding to freshmanitis are the pitfalls awaiting many star athletes emerging from high school careers where they were the cat's meow of an entire community. If a kid was friendly, smiled in class, stayed out of jail, and did not impregnate the school superintendent's daughter, chances are he received the unending adulation of most people whom he encountered. As previously mentioned, these worshippers also abound in the college environment. Assistant coaches, tutors, boosters, and cute and cuddly "jock groupies" are always available, but adoration of the athlete may no longer be unanimous. Consider the finding of a UCLA study:

> Finally, many freshmen athletes who expect college to be a continuation of their high school experience are surprised and shocked at the realization that some professors and students think less, rather than more, of them because they are athletes. Athletes who arrive on campus expecting special treatment and acceptance as important members of the academic community or student body often become aware for the first time that they are perceived as a "dumb jock," not as someone to be looked up to.[5]

In fact, 55 percent of Division I college basketball and football players have the perception that college professors do not regard them as serious students.[6] Indeed, it must be a bit harrowing to exchange the friendly smile and wink of a shop teacher upon a late arrival to class for the disdainful glance of a history professor who appears to be from another galaxy.

Other roadblocks facing student-athletes are the stringent demands upon their time. This is particularly true for players in the revenue-producing sports of football and basketball. A Division I basketball or football player spends an average of 30 hours per week in practice, preparations, and actual contests. This is the "equivalent of holding a three-quarter-time job," and it is a major reason why student-athletes report difficulty in making academics a top priority.[7]

Somehow, the kids survive. If the statistical studies are to be believed, many athletes overcome the problems of convoluted priorities, lack of self-responsibility, derecruitment, and lessened adulation. These barriers are real, though, and they should receive consideration in any reforms or improvements in the overall athletic-academic environment.

The Trials of the Minority Student-Athlete

Over and above the common obstacles facing all student-athletes are the peculiar and burdensome academic shortcomings that hinder minority or economically disadvantaged athletes. Discussed by few and understood by fewer, the educational deficiencies facing minorities and the poor, primarily the black football and basketball players, can be insurmountable. Ranging from academic to attitudinal to environmental, the harsh realities that many impoverished students bring with them from high schools or junior colleges make academic success a puzzle with no readily apparent solution. The problems of the black and/or poor student-athlete only serve to magnify the aforementioned risks related to priorities, responsibility, and athletic stress. It is a testimony to these young people's fortitude that as many of them survive the Division I jungle as do.

This country prides itself on equal opportunity for all its citizens. Politicians jump at the opportunity to woo the minority vote or appoint a prominent, like-thinking black to an administrative post. Historians cite the significance of *Brown v. Board of Education*, a landmark decision against separate-but-equal educational policies, and one that served as a watershed for minority education. Even Coca Cola and Chrysler populate television advertisements with blacks, native Americans, and Asians, providing further evidence that we live in a harmonious, pluralistic society.

Perhaps it is these modern, vividly colored commercials that paint the perceived ideal image of the American reality. Healthy, well-dressed, well-fed children, representing every imaginable race, creed, and color, cavort in a seemingly boundless suburban world bursting with readily attainable material goods. Happy families, bright green lawns, shiny new cars, and nine-room houses seem as ordinary as a summer day. Even the city is bright, clean, and sun drenched, and every urban resident has enough money for a Big Mac or a Chevrolet.

These blurry, soft, airbrushed visions are, unfortunately, more misperception than reality. Although everyone would like to believe that poverty is extinct or, at least, evaporating like puddles on a playground, the facts simply do not support the hope. Certainly, poverty does not live next door, and it cannot be found in a 30-second spiel for IBM. But poverty exists in the United States, and Michael Harrington's slap to the face of American consciousness in his book *The Other America: Poverty In The United States* is as necessary now as it was in 1962—in fact, maybe more so.

Poverty is not seen between the hedges at the University of Georgia's famed Sanford Stadium, but it is there. Poverty is a far cry from the pandemonium of the University of Arkansas' Barnhill Arena, but it is there. Poverty is the farthest thing from one's mind when the Cotton Bowl explodes in Texas orange and Oklahoma red during the Battle of the Red River, but you had better believe it is there. America's poor, the primary source of at-risk students, include a growing number of black young people. Coincidentally, NCAA Division I athletic teams have also featured many black athletes, the same athletes who experience so many of the well-publicized academic difficulties. The relationship is all too obvious, and in fact, the college-level academic woes are related more to economics than to race. This does not change the fact that the black student-athlete is often missing the mark. Be they economically generated or not, the specific academic and social problems that black and other disadvantaged athletes bring to college are worth examining.

Thrust into a world of greed and gluttony, young, impoverished blacks get to taste the hors d'oeuvres, but they rarely feast on the main course. Playing for coaches whose salaries often reach six figures, black players become part of a fairy tale, soap opera existence featuring wealthy boosters, beautiful dancing girls, and enough intrigue and scandal for a year of "General Hospital." Like the television commercials that flaunted the unattainable for most of their youthful lives, Division I sports give many poor young blacks an art gallery glimpse of a treasure that few are able to own. If economic disparity were the lone problem, college athletics might serve as a melting pot, breaking down social barriers and elevating the status of the disadvantaged. Unfortunately, the rude realities of poverty and latent racism, manifested in a deficient educational background, often interfere with what would otherwise be a golden opportunity. Some success stories do happen, and many black or culturally disadvantaged athletes have made the most of their athletic and academic chances. The Kelby Stuckey story, highlighted in chapter 1, is an excellent example, and NCAA promotional pieces are filled with tales that would make Horatio Alger proud. However, the failures and squandered chances are many, and these disappointments can usually be traced to the fact that many black and minority athletes are and have been at-risk students.

At-Risk Students

The concept of at-risk students is well documented and is the focus of much educational dialogue. Descriptions of at-risk students abound, with "developmentally delayed" and "marginal" being among the more common. Whatever the label and its exact meaning, such terms have the common denominator of identifying students who are prone to academic failure. Despite years of incessant dialogue and attention, the problem persists. Only a radical change of attitude or a massive infusion of funds will eliminate the societal tragedy of students whose success in school seems unlikely.

At-risk students are found at all educational levels. Early childhood, elementary, and secondary education are all inundated with students who lack the academic skills or environmental backgrounds necessary to achieve in the traditional public school setting. Pinpointing a single "curable" cause is difficult, and the traits of at-risk students are diverse enough to preclude the implementation of a systematic remedy. Naturally, disagreement over the relative influences of heredity and environment is prominent in attempts to define the problem. As in the chicken-and-egg debate, various educational psychologists weigh so-called "native intelligence" against Locke's tabula rasa concept, in which environment is viewed as the primary determinant. Centuries have not settled this debate, but one fact is undeniable: Children lacking in certain experiences will more than likely encounter difficulties in their schooling.

Although America's public school system is far from perfect, and though reform should be a constant consideration, the cases are rare where a motivated and academically prepared child is transformed into an unmotivated illiterate by a third-grade teacher. That is not to say that this hair-raising scenario does not occasionally occur; there are some teachers and principals whose treatment of children should unconditionally qualify them for the fate of Prometheus. But these cases are exceptions, and most schools, at least to a certain degree, facilitate some form of learning. The problems of at-risk students begin before they reach school, and at-risk traits manifest themselves as early as preschool and kindergarten. Unfortunately, the resources necessary to remedy the problems are often lacking.

Early Childhood Education

The traditional objective of preschools and kindergartens is to give young children a knowledge or experiential base that will serve as a foundation for the basic skills instruction that has historically dominated the elementary school curriculum. The problem is that a young child has already developed an experiential base, and some students enter school far behind and never narrow the gap. Experiences are education's missing link: Through experiences, children learn language, meaning, and association. "Experiences" is a somewhat nebulous concept, but the consensus among educators is that play, trips, oral and aural activities, sensory environment, and peer and family relationships all contribute to young children's experiential backgrounds. Youngsters lacking such a background may be delayed developmentally, and their performance may fall below the norm in one or more skill areas. Understanding and use of language, perception through sight and hearing, and motor development and hand-eye coordination can all be adversely affected by lack of experiences. Expressive and receptive language deficiencies are obvious outcomes of weaknesses in the experiential domain, and a child entering elementary school without prerequisite language skills is facing a long uphill climb.[8]

The prospects are not rosy for a child entering elementary school with skill deficiencies. As cruel as it may seem, eventual scholastic failure can often be predicted as early as the first grade. Sorting, placement, and ability grouping often begin in this initial year, and reading group membership with the fluently reading Bluebirds or the hesitantly stuttering Vultures is usually determined. The notion "Once a Bluebird always a Bluebird, and once a Vulture always a Vulture" usually, if regrettably, holds true.

One would like to think that schooling narrows the deficit, raising the low-achieving pupil toward the level of the more successful students. Unfortunately, just the opposite occurs. Anyone who has ever taken a graduate education course knows that the gap between successful and unsuccessful students widens as students progress through the elementary grades.

Elementary School Years

During preschool years, the problems of the at-risk student are described as experiential and perceptual. In elementary school, however, the shortcomings become more tangible. Problems in reading, writing, and mathematics may all characterize the low-achieving student; these weaknesses are usually reflected in poor grades and low standardized test scores, which also serve to substantiate a student's negative self-concept. Particularly worrisome are reading problems. Directly related to preschool language and experiential deficits, reading deficiencies may be academically lethal because reading is the prerequisite for a vast amount of future learning. This relationship is exemplified by the pivotal transition that occurs around the fourth grade, when developmental reading, or learning to read, gives way to functional reading, or reading to learn.

Now a child's reading problems are no longer exclusive to reading class. They become social studies problems, science problems, and math problems. As the reading problems multiply, it is little wonder that the proficiency gap engulfs the low-achieving students.

Massive amounts of time, resources, and energy are exhausted in the often-futile effort to combat reading deficiencies and the resulting academic problems. This frustrating situation is not due to faulty methodology but is more related to the fact that successful reading comprehension is based on prior knowledge—the ability to relate past experiences to the printed text. Overcoming years of academic struggle and experiential privation is simply too great a task for most remediation programs. This is not to say that the many excellent and committed teachers who attempt remediation do not "save" some students; they do. It is just that many low-achieving students pose problems too great for school systems mired in homogeneous practices, traditional curricula, and limited resources.

Another twist to the at-risk student dilemma also appears in the elementary school. Underachievement, where students perform below their capabilities, serves only to muddle the entire marginal student issue.[9] Sometimes temporary but often lasting, underachievement can be traced to attitude and health problems, or it may spring from home problems such as divorce, child abuse, or familial substance abuse. Such problems are extremely difficult for teachers and administrators to combat, and the underachievers and their characteristics add an entirely new dimension to the at-risk issue.[10] As Owen Bradford Butler, former chairman of Proctor and Gamble and a member of the Committee for Economic Development, stated, "Most of the high school dropouts drop out in the first grade. They never join school. They don't drop out of school; they never drop in."[11]

High School

Whereas the plight of the elementary-aged at-risk child is sad, the ramifications for marginal high school students are often tragic. This is not meant to downplay the significance of the preschool or elementary school years, where it all begins. It is just that in the realm of secondary schooling, society reaps what it has sown. Tragically, society is often a grim reaper. Truancy, dropping out, delinquency, violence, teen pregnancy, and substance abuse are all found to a greater degree among at-risk students who have become disgruntled and disenfranchised.[12]

What happens to these low-achieving and underachieving dropouts? What is the outlook for a 17-year-old unwed mother from a single-parent family where alcohol abuse may be the daily norm? What opportunities are there for young people enveloped in such tragic situations? The National Alliance of Business projects a gloomy forecast:

> The most rapidly growing, yet most vulnerable of the nation's labor pool is concentrated where schools are inferior, work ex-

perience opportunities are poorest, and available full-time jobs are declining. Although business will need these workers, they will not be prepared to work and will too often find jobs inaccessible to public transportation. Many potential workers will turn to welfare; some will turn to crime. There, individuals will be a drain on society and will be lost as consumers of business' products and services.[13]

Such are the prospects for the at-risk student. Although the National Alliance of Business viewpoint is somewhat reactionary and economic in nature, it does acknowledge the basic survival problem facing today's high school washouts.

Society's Shared Responsibility

Placing the blame on any single sector of society is virtually impossible. Every person, to a certain degree, must shoulder the responsibility when young children are systematically deemed failures and after a 10- to 12-year period are discarded like assembly line rejects. Still, the American school's role has to be examined. Large-group instruction, narrow instructional techniques, differential treatment of ability groups, misuse of evaluation, and inequitable funding are common educational practices that reinforce and aggravate at-risk students' marginality.[14] Robert L. Sinclair and Ward J. Ghory, in their excellent book *Reaching Marginal Students: A Primary Concern for School Renewal*, described the schools' inertia, which frustrates the gains of at-risk students:

> Schools often permit a significant degree of marginality—that is, disconnections between students and the conditions designed for learning. In other words, schools allow individuals or subgroups to develop and sustain faulty or incomplete relationships with other school members and programs. For a complex combination of reasons most schools tolerate the existence of a fringe population that is not fully involved in the mainstream of school life. These marginal students learn and contribute only a fraction of what they can and thus use only a portion of their potential at school.[15]

Schools are not the only culprits, and there are times when individuals—at-risk kids, for instance—simply make bad decisions that hinder their own progress. It should also be remembered that preschools and kindergartens have no control over a child's first 3 years, and there is not a psychologist (behaviorist, humanist, or cognitivist) who will deny the extraordinary impact of a child's early formative years. The home environment plays a tremendous role in future development. When different at-risk or marginal students are examined, more often than not a common trait is found—poverty.

The Disastrous Effects of Poverty

Poverty may be the largest piece in the at-risk puzzle. Low-income children are more likely to reside in homes where the warning signs of potential school failure—health problems, child abuse, unemployment, substance abuse, and violence—are more prevalent.[16] Even if these negative influences were missing, low-income parents might be unable to provide the experiences and advantages that middle-income or upper-income children enjoy. This discrepancy is inherently unfair, but there is no denying that "the greatest predictor of educational success is family income of the student," and that "poverty is the greatest predictor of failure."[17]

That poor children struggle in school is hardly a revelation. Settlement houses, prevalent from 1890 to 1910, recognized the relationship between poverty and educational failure; they attempted to aid the massive flood of immigrants trying to adjust to a strange culture. President Lyndon Johnson's Great Society spawned the Head Start, Follow Through, and Title I programs, all of which endeavored to improve education for children from low-income families.[18] The problems still exist, however. While Head Start programs currently serve some 400,000 children, at least 3 million more are eligible.[19]

America's downtrodden are an eclectic aggregation, but some groups have historically had, and continue to have, greater representation. Whereas two of three impoverished youngsters are white, "the percentage of black children living with one parent who are poor is much higher, and those children who stay in poverty for more than four years (only one in three poor children does) are heavily black."[20] Also indicative of the American poverty infrastructure is the rapid increase in the number of poverty-level households headed by a black or Hispanic female. "Ninety percent of the increase of children born into poverty is in these households."[21] Particularly disturbing are the age-related demographics of poverty. Today, a child under age 6 is six times more likely to be poor than an American over age 65. This means that nearly half of the poor in the United States are children and that the number of at-risk youngsters has increased by over 2 million since the beginning of the 1980s. Compounding the problems represented by these figures is that fact that the country's black and Hispanic populations will nearly double by the year 2020.[22]

Language: Bridge or Barrier?

An entire new mode of communication awaits freshmen from the inner city or the rural South, and inappropriate language skills may very well be the primary factor in frustrating and eventually dooming some minority athletes in their attempts to succeed academically. Verbal, reading, and writing skills may be lacking, or they may suggest skew lines, where neither the language of the student nor that of the institution is necessarily superior, but they simply do not connect.

In the years between 1982 and 1986, when Oklahoma State University prepared to play Oklahoma University in football or basketball, the Oklahoma State campus radio station would broadcast fictitious interviews with prominent black OU athletes who would participate in the upcoming contests. The typical interview would go something like this:

> **Interviewer:** Well, Mr. Tisdale, what are your thoughts on the upcoming game?
>
> **Tisdale:** Ugah bugah hoogaloo ugh ugh.
>
> **Interviewer:** Really—would you share your thoughts on your coach, Billy Tubbs?
>
> **Tisdale:** I be, you be, we be, yo' mama!

These supposedly comical interludes were quite popular, and, unfortunately, they probably reflect the white majority's mass perception of the language abilities of black student-athletes. Coaches, athletic directors, and school administrators often cringe when a well-known black athlete is interviewed by the media, and an articulate black athlete will earn postgame cocktail party praise from the alumni for "talking real good."

Although the United States is a linguistically pluralistic nation, its language diversity pales when compared to that of other nations. India, for example, has more than 20 languages and 80 dialects; in the Soviet Union, there are more than 200 languages spoken and well over 1,000 variations and dialects.[23] This is not to say that language in the U.S. does not feature diversity; it does. One of the more prevalent dialects is black English. A dialect is a social or regional variation in a language, and a dialect becomes nonstandard when it differs from the primary dialects used by the general population.[24] Black English is labeled as nonstandard, in contrast to, say, southern English, which is simply perceived as a regional dialect.[25] This discrepancy occurs because widespread regional Caucasian dialects are generally accepted, whereas the social group dialect of blacks and the isolated regional variations of Cajun, Appalachian, and Hawaiian English are "socially unacceptable, or non-standard."[26]

An example of the difference in acceptance between a regional dialect and a nonstandard dialect is the word "y'all," extremely common in southern English. When my family moved from the Chicago area to Greensboro, North Carolina, during my junior high years, I was stunned that "y'all" was used in school by teachers and principal alike. On the other hand, I distinctly remember many of my black peers being reprimanded for using their form of nonstandard English in the same classroom.

SAT Vocabulary

Question No. 1:   Melodeon is to organist as:
- A)   reveille is to burglar
- B)   solo is to accompanist
- C)   crescendo is to pianist
- D)   anthem is to choirmaster
- E)   kettle drum is to tympanist

Tony Williams, a 6'5", 275-pound black defensive lineman from St. Louis responded, "I don't know what that is" when asked to describe a melodeon, and he had "no idea" what a tympanist was either.

Question No. 2:   The opposite of antediluvian is:
- A)   homemade
- B)   jingoistic
- C)   newfangled
- D)   well-balanced
- E)   sweet-scented

"I read kind of slow," said Lamont Head, a highly recruited football player from Pattonville, Missouri. "I run out of time on the test. And some of the history questions really get me, and the language, the vocabulary. I'm no dummy, though. I know I can do the college work, because I work hard."[a]

The two questions (difficult for the best of students) are samples from a recent SAT,* and they and the athletes' responses to them are indicative of the language barriers many minority athletes encounter as they enter institutions of higher education. The ACT and the SAT are the initial shock, but they are mere foreshadowings of the hurdles to come.

Note. [a]Mike Eisenbath, "Test of Your Life," *St. Louis Post-Dispatch*, 2 February 1989, D-3. *The answer to question No. 1 is E; the correct response for No. 2 is C.

Although social dialects are "well-ordered, highly structured, highly developed language systems"[27] and black English "possesses its own vocabulary, pronunciation, and syntax,"[28] a child immersed in a black English environment will inevitably encounter language-related academic difficulties at some time during his or her schooling. The best way to approach the education of these black-English-speaking students is a continuing source of pedagogical controversy.

Approaches to Nonstandard Dialects

The three current approaches to eradicating, keeping, or adding to a child's natural dialect each receive support and criticism.

Eradication Approach

The eradiction approach advocates eliminating black English and nonstandard dialects and replacing them with the more acceptable and widely used regional dialect. A child's language is constantly corrected to bring it into line with the standard style.[29] The rationale for this approach is that functionality in standard English is a prerequisite for success in the academic and business worlds. There are, however, many problems inherent in this approach. Students are made to feel inferior about their language, and they may become reluctant to speak in school. This undoubtedly is a major reason why many black athletes are hesitant to participate verbally in their college classes. Another problem is that black English is part of a black person's culture; in requiring a complete change in dialect, schools may erode the black culture altogether.[30]

"Keep" Approach

Operating under the opposite assumption is the "keep" approach, which views every dialect as having equal communication potential and being part of a living culture. The "keep" proponents feel that no young person should be required to write or speak in a dialect different from the one he or she has acquired and that the dialect a child brings to school should be treated as a perfectly acceptable means of communication. Like the eradication approach, however, this approach is fraught with disadvantages. Few written materials are published in nonstandard syntax and vocabulary, and students who wish to read widely "must know how to interpret the syntax and vocabulary of the standard form."[31] Also, as was stated in support of the eradication approach, nonstandard dialects are not normally used in business or "proper" social situations, and teachers may simply not understand them.

"Add" Approach

The third approach is to add standard English abilities to the repertoires of nonstandard-English-speaking students. Students are allowed or even encouraged to communicate in their own dialect, but at the same time, they are encouraged to learn standard English so they can properly function in situations where that form is prevalent. There are obvious contradictions in teaching students bidialectal skills, however. How will students become proficient at something they don't use daily at home? How will they develop the subtle ability to know when to "turn on" and "turn off" a particular dialect? Despite these difficult questions, the bidialectal skill approach is the most popular one,[32] and it represents an attitude of "let's just do the best we can." As Clarence Underwood, Jr., assistant commissioner for the Big Ten, urges, academicians should "not allow jargon, colloquialisms, slang, or substandard English to deter them from making a genuine effort to communicate with black student athletes."[33] For baffled and frustrated professors, and for black student-athletes already isolated by purpose, appearance, and now language, Mr. Underwood's advice may be more easily stated than followed.

Language barriers and the educational efforts to overcome them are not limited to blacks. Mexican-Americans, Vietnamese, poor whites from Appalachia, and many others among our nation's minorities and disenfranchised face the same communication-related obstacles. If these groups' speaking and listening skills were the only associated problems, the language and dialect question would loom large enough. Saddeningly, though, like dominos in a row, one educational disadvantage leads to another, and oral language deficiencies often lead to something perhaps even more tragic—illiteracy.

Literacy

"Of the 159 members of the United Nations, the U.S. ranks 49th in its level of literacy."[34] One report indicates that 25 million Americans "cannot read the poison warning on a can of pesticide," and an additional 35 million do not read at a level necessary for survival in today's society.[35] Another study claims that 27 million Americans cannot read above the fourth-grade level, and these citizens struggle with traffic signs, medicine bottle labels, notes from their children's teachers, and instructions on job applications. Of the 8 million unemployed in 1982, 75 percent lacked literacy skills prerequisite for on-the-job training. It is estimated that 75 percent of incarcerated offenders are illiterate.[36]

Obviously, the illiteracy problem is a national disgrace, and there is no end to its negative ramifications. The statistics and tragedies could fill reams, but they would provide no revelations. Educators, business people, and some politicians are all too aware of America's illiterates. But, as with homelessness and other poverty-related calamities, if the problem does not actually hit home, answers are usually lacking. Public awareness has even reached the point where 1987 was designated the Year of the Reader, and a national movement known as Youth 2000 has fingered illiteracy as a serious threat to the national economy and the future employability of today's youth. These publicity campaigns have been successful to a point. The media blitz surrounding the Year of the Reader campaign reportedly has increased citizen awareness of functional illiteracy from 21.4 percent to 30 percent,[37] and the Youth 2000 movement has resulted in the formation of business-education literacy advocacy partnerships across the United States. Still, many literacy advocates are skeptical of any tangible gains. As Nancy Larrick, author of *A Parent's Guide to Children's Reading*, states, "I have seen no claim that functional illiteracy has declined as a result. Nor do I expect to."[38]

Causes of Illiteracy

The causes of illiteracy are numerous. Poverty, lack of reading in the home, learning disabilities, dropping out of school, and even the schools themselves have been cited as playing primary roles in the illiteracy epidemic. Some view the schools as the ultimate culprit. The traditional public school environment and its alienation of the at-risk student has already been discussed. Many reading instruction researchers blame widespread teaching methodologies for the current lack of reading interest and skills. Often described as mechanized, most elementary schools' reading curricula incorporate basal readers that feature condensed stories using limited vocabulary and more limited imagination. Inundated with fill-in-the-blank workbooks and computer-aided instruction, these current approaches immerse students in systematic phonics programs where initial reading experiences center on such fanciful topics as the sounds of vowels and consonant clusters. Bombarded with blasé stories read in assembly line fashion and tedious work in mundane, repetitive workbooks, "it is no wonder that American children (ages 6–11) rush home from school to watch a weekly average of 23 hours and 19 minutes of television, year round."[39]

The mechanistic approach to reading instruction appeals to neither teacher nor student, but tradition and administrative and peer pressure compel many elementary teachers to stay the basal reader course, even though many of them have been taught and know better. According to Nancy Larrick, "teachers are not directed to read aloud each day from good literature. Nor are they expected to draw children into recording or dictating their responses to experiences or situations. Oral language—the natural language of everyday speech—is not provided for children to read."[40] Maybe it is this neglect of oral language that is so detrimental to the reading skills of many young black students. Speaking nonstandard English at home and with friends, young blacks are expected to learn to read with materials written in a language different from their own. Add this language dichotomy to the inherent boredom of the reading program, and it is no surprise that blacks and other minority students are those most afflicted with illiteracy.

Breadth of the Problem

Although English-speaking whites make up nearly 77 percent of America's total population, the U.S. Department of Education estimates that only 41 percent of America's illiterates are white English speakers. (See

Table 3.1   Illiteracy Rates by Ethnic Group

Group	Percent of total population	Share of illiterates (%)
White English speakers	77	41
Black English speakers	12	22
Spanish speakers	8	22
Others	3	15

Source: U.S. Department of Labor. *Youth 2000: Challenge and Opportunity.* Prepared by the Hudson Institute. June 1986, 18.

Table 3.1.) These figures represent a significant discrepancy in levels of literacy and are undoubtedly related to the high poverty levels of blacks and other minorities.

It would be a gross overgeneralization to say that all black, minority, or poor student-athletes enter college as functional illiterates. Some do, though, and many more enter higher education with handicapping reading deficiencies. My experiences as an athletic academic adviser at Southwest Missouri State University are indicative of the widespread problem. During a 3-year period, our basketball program recruited eight black players, all of whom had graduated from junior colleges. I tested five of these eight players to determine their reading levels. Not one of these tested read above the eighth-grade level; one young man had a reading level that was significantly lower. Whether or not this range of test scores translates into illiteracy is a moot point. The fact is that whether illiterate, functionally illiterate, or borderline literate—whatever the label—these five athletes were going to struggle with college reading material.

Read a randomly selected paragraph from John A. Garraty's *The American Nation*, a text that is used widely in basic American history classes and is typical of many college textbooks:

> For most laborers, the working day still tended to approximate the hours of daylight, but it was shortening perceptibly by the 1880's. In 1860 the average was 11 hours, by 1880 one labored more than 10, and radicals were beginning to talk about 8 hours as a fair day's work. To some extent the exhausting pace of the new factories made longer hours uneconomical, but employers realized this slowly, and until they did, many workers suffered.[41]

This paragraph is hardly verbose, and its points are made directly and succinctly. However, according to the Raygor Readability Estimator, the text is written on the "Professional" level, which is the highest level after the "College" and "Twelfth" grade levels. Regardless of its actual level, words like *approximate, perceptibly, radicals,* and *exhausting* may pose problems for less skilled readers, not to mention students on the literacy borderline. These very same students may be—and probably are—intellectually capable of comprehending the meaning of the words. However, words on the printed page, while comprehensible in spoken language, may be as mysterious as hieroglyphics to students with reading problems.

Literacy in the Future

Despite the good motives behind the Year of the Reader and Youth 2000, literacy will probably not become universal among American citizens by the next century. And despite the efforts of reading instruction experts, who are urging administrators and teachers to view the teaching of reading in an entirely different light, many student-athletes will continue to encounter great difficulties in meeting the reading demands of a college curriculum. Even if a methodological revolution were to occur in the stodgy, publisher-dominated world of reading education, many young students, bogged down in poverty and lacking experiential prior knowledge, would not find functional literacy an easy achievement.

Although it is obvious that reading deficiencies compound the academic difficulties faced by many economically disadvantaged college students, it is virtually impossible to measure the extent of this problem on a nationwide basis. The reliability of reading tests and examiners varies from one institution to another. Nonetheless, simple logic allows one to see the negative scholastic ramifications of poor reading skills, and there is no doubt that many student-athletes' best academic efforts have been thwarted by frustrating reading disabilities. Unfortunately, development of other important skills is retarded by the same factors affecting verbal and reading skills.

Writing Skills

Communication is based on a hierarchy of language abilities. At the bottom of the hierarchy is listening, and above that are the skills of speaking, reading, and writing. Not coincidentally, this hierarchy reflects the order in which various communication abilities are developed. A youngster learns to listen, then to speak, and—one hopes—to read and to write. The expressive communication skills depend upon the receptive abilities: Thus a child with a hearing disability will often have trouble with speech development, and reading problems usually signal difficulties in writing.

Understanding these relationships sheds light on the academic difficulties experienced by many black and minority athletes. Saddled (from the perspective of a standard English advocate) with a nonstandard dialect and often lagging in reading proficiency, many minority and economically disadvantaged students, all too predictably, have subpar writing skills. There is a cruel aspect to this situation, too. Although verbal deficiencies can be hidden if one remains quiet, and a reading problem may be apparent only to the reader, poor writing skills are there in black and white for the world to see. How hard it must be to hand in a paper knowing that the professor may shake his or her head in disbelief and dash to the nearest faculty lounge ranting, ''I can't believe so-and-so was admitted to this institution. His writing skills are terrible!''

The writing problems of many student-athletes are remarkably similar to their difficulties in reading. As previously discussed, writing and reading are related, and ''comprehending and composing occur interchangeably''[42] as students use language to construct meaning. Reading difficulties may reflect nonstandard English and a limited experiential base, and writing problems are usually compounded by reading difficulties.

Nonstandard English and poor reading skills are not the only factors associated with marginal writing abilities. Many educators cite inadequate and antiquated instructional methods as a prime determinant. These writers, teachers, and researchers recognize the weakness of the traditional English curriculum in which the mechanics of writing are taught separately from the act of writing. Although universities and colleges have long acknowledged the writing deficiencies of students, their attempts at remediation have often been mired in the same traditional grammar-based practices that provided inadequate instruction to poor writers in the first place. Faced with a learning environment in which they have previously experienced failure, students often lack the intrinsic motivation and effort to make any real progress in developing their writing abilities.[43]

Extrinsic motivation is also a problem with many universities' remedial English programs. My institution, Southwest Missouri State, used to offer a 1-credit-hour remedial English course for students who had scored 13 or below on the ACT English subtest or who had failed an English proficiency exam in their freshman composition classes. These students were required to pass the remedial class before they could enroll or reenroll in freshman composition. Unfortunately, the remedial class had the ''Bonehead English'' stigma, and students received neither a grade nor credit toward any degree program. Obviously, the lack of grade and credit diminished a student's desire to strive for success, and the remedial class was erroneously perceived as a punitive ordeal. This attitude was particularly prevalent among the many student-athletes required to take the course, and it led to some of them floundering in the course for two or three semesters before they were allowed to enter the standard composition classes. Fortunately, our English department recently revamped its program in a way that provides more motivation for less-skilled writers.

Read Between the Lines

Read the following short essay by a black college basketball player who was keeping his head above academic water through hard work and sincere effort.

> My favorite part of the city is going to Springs Park. When I go to the park I enjoy feeding the birds, and just sitting in the sunshine. The park is filled with a variety of toys for kids for instunt their are slides, swingset, merrygoround tennis court, basketball court all of these toys can be found at the park. I like to go to the park and Relax and easy my mind.
>
> The Springs Park is open to the public. anyone can go to the park. when I go to the park I try to go alone that way I can enjoy myself more I want have to worry about know one else. If you go to the park alone you better be careful, because their is alot of crazy people out there. So I advise you if you get lonely go by and visit the Springs Park, you want be lonely then.

This student-athlete, who scored over 700 on his combined SAT, expressed himself honestly. If the reader mentally supplies the proper punctuation, the essay becomes readable. Unfortunately for the writer, most readers, especially college professors, do not want to mentally supply punctuation. Subject-verb disagreements, run-on sentences, and spelling and punctuation errors do not a passing paper make. The problem lies in the fact that the student wrote his essay exactly as he speaks; he simply never mastered formal standard English. A more detailed analysis of the essay reveals it to be equivalent to a "marginally competent" fifth-grade essay. A fifth-grade writing level would be slightly below this student's seventh-grade reading level; with writing being the final communication skill to be mastered, the fifth-grade assessment is probably quite accurate,[a] and in all likelihood is common to many student-athletes from similar backgrounds.

Note. [a]V.A. Bayliss and N.L. Walker, *Bayliss/Walker Scales: Holistic Writing Evaluation Grades 1–6* (Springfield, MO: Southwest Missouri State University, 1988).

Content Areas

Adequate proficiency in basic communication skills is often a prerequisite for success in other disciplines, and many low-income minority students consequently struggle in the content areas, particularly in math and the natural and social sciences. The discrepancies between the math and science scores of black students and nonminority students begin showing up early in the elementary school years. Although the gap has been narrowed slightly during the last 2 decades, a clear delineation between black and nonminority achievement in math and science still exists.[44] This discrepancy persists and often widens during the secondary years, and it is reflected in the ACT and SAT scores of entering college students.

Mathematics

Achieving success in mathematics has been particularly difficult for some minorities. The average ACT math subtest scores for blacks (11.0) and Mexican-Americans (13.7) are far below the average score of 18 for non-minorities.* SAT scores also illustrate the problem, as the scores for blacks (377) and Mexican-Americans (424) on the mathematics portion of the test are again significantly lower than the average score (489) for whites.[45] Some blacks do so poorly on the mathematics part of the SAT that one educational statistician suggested that "perhaps 15% of the blacks who took the math SAT in 1983 would have scored higher if they had left the test blank or filled it out entirely at random."[46] The reasoning behind this statement was that so many black examinees scored below the chance level on the math SAT that the test makers had to "calculate negative raw scores in order to achieve a 'normal' (bell-shaped) distribution of scaled scores."[47]

The Sciences

Although the proficiency gap may be slightly narrower than in math, blacks and Mexican-Americans continue to fare poorly in the social studies and natural sciences content areas (see Table 3.2). Failure to score well in the social studies and science domains is undoubtedly related to and compounded by reading problems and the lack of an adequate experiential base. Reading, as was previously mentioned, is transformed from a developmental learning activity to a functional skill in about the fourth grade. Students with poor reading skills are caught in an educational quandary, as learning and mastery in social studies and science often become extremely textbook oriented. At a time when these students need additional reading instruction, the time spent on developmental reading often diminishes. Although this is a misguided and unfortunate pedagogical state of affairs, many public school curricula are text dominated. This is a veritable stamp of failure for the language-deficient youngster.

A lack of the experiences that add up to "cultural literacy" is also a major barrier to minority students' success in social studies and science.

---

*Scores on the SAT range from 200 to 800 on each of the two parts, with the mean score for college-bound students being 500. For the ACT, the scores range from 1 to 36 for the total test, with the mean for college-bound students being 20.

Table 3.2   ACT Scores in the Sciences by Race

Race	Social studies	Natural science
Black	12.1	15.7
Mexican-American	13.9	17.9
White	18.3	22.2

Source: "Students From Most Minority Groups Improve Scores on College Admission Tests This Year; Average Stable," *The Chronicle of Higher Education*, 30 September 1987, 1.

The general recent knowledge necessary for cultural literacy is missing for many American youths, particularly those from families whose income levels prohibit vacations and other culturally enlightening experiences. Once again, the problem comes full circle, and educators are faced with the stark academic contrasts "between people whose families have a lot of money and people whose families don't."[48]

Computer Literacy

A lack of computer competency hampers many black and disadvantaged student-athletes in their scholastic endeavors. One black basketball player, a junior college transfer attending Southwest Missouri State University, expressed dismay at being asked to work on a skills preparation series in a university computer lab. Explaining the source of his trepidation, the student replied, "I've never been in a computer lab, much less worked at a computer!" Many public schools in inner cities or poor rural regions cannot afford expensive computer technology, and computer illiteracy may not be problematic for an underfunded school's student until he or she starts college or begins an income-producing career. In these situations, however, students without computer literacy may find themselves at a distinct disadvantage relative to those from more affluent backgrounds.

By 1990, the United States had spent $1 billion on computerized learning, but two-thirds of that amount was spent by well-to-do parents on their own children.[49] Even though the computer education age is in relative infancy, the familiar gap between the haves and have nots is already apparent. A study by the National Assessment of Educational Progress titled "Computer Competence: The First National Assessment" found that "white students scored five percent to eight percent higher than blacks and Hispanics, mainly because of greater access to computers at home and in school."[50] If public school systems continue to falter in developing their own computer education programs, the less affluent students may suffer an "irreparable educational disadvantage."[51]

Part of the computer literacy boom is no more than crass commercialism and jumping on the educational bandwagon. One humorist even wrote, "Studying computer hardware is as essential to its effective use as studying the innards of your TV is to effective television watching."[52] Although there is more truth to that statement than an IBM marketing wizard would like to admit, the fact remains that computers and the knowledge to manage them have become an integral part of America's economic and educational activity. It would be yet another example of the inequities of American society if the maldistribution of resources doomed certain segments of the population to remain unskilled in an area of vital importance to their economic and educational well-being.

Test-Taking Skills

Though "what you know" is the primary issue, "proving to others what you know" is becoming an important ploy in the academic success game. Test-taking skills have become more and more significant with the advent of stricter exit and entrance requirements and the fact that thousands of dollars in academic and athletic scholarships often depend on the quantitative results of a single exam. College texts, self-help books, continuing education programs, and private tutorial services that build test-taking skills have sprouted like daisies as a wide variety of educational entrepreneurs attempt to capitalize on a profitable trend. And their efforts work, too. Students who complete, for instance, a computer-assisted exam preparation series have been found to raise their scores significantly, as much as 4 to 6 points, on the ACT test. Unfortunately, though, not all students have access to such programs.

The consensus among educators is that low-income minority students have poor test-taking skills and lack what is commonly called "test readiness." Research indicates that minorities, particularly blacks, lack test readiness because students from low socioeconomic groups are less test-wise (thanks to experiential factors, modeling, etc.) and experience more test anxiety. Research findings also suggest that many tests are likely to be biased against minorities, particularly blacks.[53] The problem is so acute that the 1986 annual meeting of the National Alliance of Black School Educators in Washington, DC, stressed the need to teach black children how to pass tests. Any gains in this area, it was stated, would result only from systematic efforts.[54]

The Pro Myth

"I wouldn't go back to Altgeld Gardens. At Altgeld—everybody is just hanging out."

Caleb Davis, former Division I
basketball player from Chicago's
George Washington Carver High School

"Why doesn't that kid want a college degree? Doesn't he know that a degree is his ticket out?" These questions, often asked by those steeped in the values of the white middle class, seem legitimate enough. Why would a student-athlete from a disadvantaged background squander his golden opportunity to obtain a "free" college degree and make himself a useful and productive member of society? Well, the so-called squandering is not always by the athlete's choice, and the usually successful people asking these questions should consider their likely reactions if they were asked to abandon home and background in order to "better" themselves and become part of what might seem an alien society. If Caleb Davis does obtain a college degree, just what will he do with it if he returns to Altgeld Gardens, where unemployment is high and gang violence is not unusual? Of course, Caleb could remain in Springfield, Missouri, but why would a black kid raised in Chicago want to stay in a medium-sized midwestern town where the population is 99 percent white and most of a person's time is spent driving up and down fast-food-laden thoroughfares listening to country music stations?

The notions of motivation and role models are rarely discussed in relation to intercollegiate athletics and academics. Although many white educators realize that these are strong undercurrents in the issue, they often avoid discussion of these factors so as not to imply a racist or culturally superior attitude. Feeling that open acknowledgment of these matters would be misinterpreted, they keep their heads in the sand and their mouths shut. Though this may be the safe route, it precludes any meaningful dialogue on the topic.

The black sociologist Harry Edwards has, however, tackled these issues head-on. Edwards believes that the attitudes and expectations of black families must change before any progress in the academic-athletic arena can be realized. He cites a UCLA study that found black families to be "four times more likely than white families to view their children's involvement in community sport as a 'start in athletic activity that may lead to a career in professional sports.' "[55] This represents, in Edwards's words, what is tantamount to a "pro myth." Unfortunately, rewards and professional opportunities simply do not exist for most student-athletes. Consider the facts: Only around "8 percent of the draft-eligible student athletes in collegiate basketball, baseball, and football are actually drafted by professional teams each year," and a mere "2 percent of the athletes drafted will ever sign professional contracts."[56] The athlete who is fortunate enough to become professional will probably have a short-lived career. Approximately 60 percent of professional players have careers that last just 3 to 4 years. Even if professional athletics is recognized as a viable and attainable career option, Edwards has estimated that with all of professional sports and related employment opportunities, fewer than 2,400 black Americans earn their living in professional sports.[57] So, although mega-bucks and stardom are appealing and may seem a quick ticket out of economic deprivation, the odds against achieving those things remove them from the realm of reality.

Dreams of the Student Athlete

Dreams

Hold fast to dreams
For if dreams die
Life is a broken-winged bird
That cannot fly.

Hold fast to dreams
For when dreams go
Life is a barren field
Frozen with snow.

Langston Hughes

Dreams may be all that some student-athletes have, and hoping and striving for stardom is not in itself a bad thing. Still, the pro myth can undercut the pursuit of other goals, and, sadly, it is not the only attitudinal problem Edwards finds in black American society. He believes that education and legitimate academic standards must receive more emphasis in the home. Black families, Edwards urges, "must instill black youths with values stressing the priority of educational achievement over athletic participation and even proficiency."[58] Finally, Edwards hits hard but true with the following statement:

> The bottom line here is that if black student athletes fail to take an active role in establishing and legitimatizing a priority upon academic achievement, nothing done by any other party to this American sports tragedy will matter if for no other reason than the fact that a slave cannot be freed against his will.[59]

What factors have led to the lack of academic motivation in many black homes is hard to say. Certainly, funding problems, lack of connection between a college degree and a good job, inadequate high school counseling programs, and the real or imaginary job ceiling as perceived by blacks and other minorities all contribute to an erosion or absence of academic motivation.

Is Opportunity Knocking?

The unavailability of funding for higher education may have powerful implications for low-income blacks. There is no denying the impact of

Ronald Reagan's economic policies. In 1980, people living in poverty paid 1.9 percent of their income in taxes, whereas 1984 found the same group paying 10.1 percent. The same period saw college tuitions increase by 12 percent, and existing grants covered less of higher education's rising cost.[60] Obviously, the growing gap between costs and resources discourages scholastic aspiration and limits access to higher education.

Compiling figures on minority access to higher education is somewhat tricky because, as Harold L. Hodgkinson of the Institute for Educational Leadership writes, "The range and diversity of higher education in the U.S. is a source of constant amazement—entering freshmen at some institutions know more than graduating seniors from others."[61] With such a wide variance in the caliber of colleges and universities, any meaningful monitoring of the progress of blacks and minorities must focus on their inroads into different types of higher education institutions. Community colleges, for instance, "have a disproportionate enrollment of black and Hispanic students," and "blue chip" institutions such as University of California, Berkeley (only 56 percent white) and Harvard (20 percent minority) have been able to increase minority enrollments and maintain high admission standards.[62] Other public and private universities, though, have not realized gains in minority student enrollment; this is a curious finding in that the high school graduation rates for blacks increased 29 percent from 1975 to 1982. Further complicating the picture is a decline in college enrollment during that 7-year period of 11 percent for blacks and 16 percent for Hispanics. Echoing these statistics somewhat are reports that between 1978 and 1985, blacks were the only minority group to realize a decline in the number of BA degrees received. They also experienced reductions in MA and PhD degrees during the same period.[63]

Hodgkinson maintains that the pertinent question is, "Why isn't higher education more appealing to America's minority high school graduates?"[64] Inadequate funding, poor counseling, and lack of job guarantee have already been presented as hypothetical reasons. Employers' postsecondary training programs and the high-tech preparations offered by the military may be viewed by minorities as appealing alternatives to higher education. Still, there is no denying the significance of role models and motivation. Considering exorbitant black dropout rates and the number of black students who come from families that include no college graduates, it may be no wonder that many eligible black youths do not attend college or enroll only to struggle and eventually cop out.

Dropping Out and Copping Out

Blacks, like all groups in American society, have experienced strong growth in high school graduation rates during this century. The population as a whole saw graduation rates of less than 50 percent in 1946 grow to approximately 73 percent in the mid-1980s, and blacks and other minorities improved their lot as well.[65] However, the early to mid-1980s also saw the back-to-basics revolution initiate an agenda of reform. The reforms strengthened secondary school academic requirements through mandated core curricula, skill mastery, and standardized exit tests. The idea was that school had become too soft, and the way to reform it was to delete the fluff and get down to the nuts and bolts of learning. The reforms (30 states increased graduation requirements in English, math, and science), of course, were successful in that schooling became more difficult. This was evidenced by the national surge in dropout rates after the advent of the reform era. Of course, ascertaining whether or not students are learning more is, unfortunately, a little more difficult, but the well-documented dropout statistics are proof that, indeed, secondary school learning has become more treacherous.

Poverty has already been identified as the greatest single predictor of educational failure, and probably no other manifestation of educational failure has the ramifications and finality of dropping out. Dropping out is an end, a nowhere, a surrender to hopelessness. It is giving in to the system, and it is synonymous with young people's admitting that organized society holds no place for them. Dropouts have been pinpointed as the greatest threat to the nation's future economy, and the numbers are growing.[66]

At least 700,000 students drop out of high school each year. Poor and minority youths are most likely to leave school, with dropout rates in some low-income communities reaching the 40 percent level.[67] In fact, Chicago (43 percent), East Los Angeles (58 percent), Washington (45 percent), and Boston (50 percent) reportedly have dropout rates exceeding that astonishingly high level.[68] These communities' public school systems are known for their large minority representation, and a Chicago sample found that the dropout rates of 47 percent for Hispanics and 45 percent for blacks were significantly greater than the 34 percent rate for whites.[69] National figures show smaller discrepancies (see Table 3.3), but the differences between whites and minorities and between the poor and nonpoor are still startling.

In the urban ghettos, nonschool problems—broken homes, drug and alcohol abuse, and violence—contribute to school dropouts and are greatest where minority students are concentrated.[70] Other school-related factors, however, have also been cited as determinants in the dropout syndrome. A student's age and reading ability both have been identified as variables that are reliable predictors of dropping out. Overage students, those who have been held back in the elementary grades, are far more likely to drop out than students of typical age. It was also found that more students who read at a fifth-grade level or below during their eighth-grade year would eventually drop out.[71]

Table 3.3   Dropout Status of Minority and Poor Youth

Group	Dropout rate (%)
Hispanic	18
Black	17
White	12
Low socioeconomic status	17
High socioeconomic status	5

Source: Tim O'Connor, "Widespread Problem Takes Toll on Students' Lives and Society," *Kansas City Times*, 23 May 1988, A-6.

Is there a sense of group hopelessness among the minority poor, or do these statistics merely reflect the frustration of young individuals? One would have to suspect that a group mind-set exists, one in which school and studies are perceived as irrelevant and futile. This would partially explain the proliferation of Edwards's pro myth, as flickering a hope as it may be. The activities of adolescents are trendy, imitative, even mythic, and the annual growth of the low-income minority dropout rate is indeed frightful. As District of Columbia school board member Eugene Kinlow said in response to local media reports that students were being teased for doing well in school, "We have to turn around the negative peer pressure."[72]

Collegiate student-athletes, naturally, are not high school dropouts. They have graduated from high school and entered the ranks, prepared or unprepared, of the scholarly elite. However, for the poor black student-athlete, athletic endeavors may have been the sole reason for staying in school. Said Caleb Davis, the soft-spoken Chicagoan, "I like to think I would have graduated and gone to college. But my talent in basketball is what allowed those things to happen."

As Eugene Kinlow pointed out, the peer pressure is often negative; positive academic role models are lacking. Herein lies the problem. Many student-athletes salvage a high school diploma through sheer doggedness or cleverness, or as grateful beneficiaries. Academics may not be an individual priority because they are not a group priority. Unfortunately, the personal priorities held by these student-athletes are not conducive to success in college. As the unmovable force of postsecondary academic pressure meets the weak, tentative, and easily swayed academic goals of the student-athlete, it is easy to predict the outcome.

What student-athletes tell coaches, academic advisers, and the media is sometimes different from what they tell themselves and each other.

Most academic advisers have never met a student-athlete, black or white, who did not at least profess a desire to graduate and do well in school. This is true. *Nobody* wants to make F's. *Nobody* wants to flunk out of school. *Nobody* wants to do these things any more than a child wishes to be a poor reader. However, for many athletes, saying they want to do well in school is like the fat man claiming he is going to lose 20 pounds as he chows down on a Taco Bell Burrito Supreme and guzzles a beer. Saying and doing are entirely different things.

The dichotomy between saying and doing may be even more pronounced with student-athletes. When a kid enters a typical Division I program, it does not take him long to figure out the score. Differentiating the "bad-ass" coaches from the lax ones, warming up to generous boosters, and defining a peer group are all taken care of in short order. It is the latter, the peer group, that may have a substantial effect on a player's attitude toward academics. If the program is one where many black players struggle academically and fail to graduate, academics may be perceived by a black athlete as a necessary evil, merely endured to ensure eligibility. In this scenario, schoolwork is treated as a scam, cheating may be prevalent, and the easiest and quickest options will usually be considered first.

Not all student-athletes, even in such a situation, throw in the scholarly towel so early. Many kids sincerely want to succeed academically and give what they honestly feel is their best effort. "Feel," though, is the key word. A student from a JUCO (junior college) often discovers that what he perceives to be his best shot is not enough. Many times a student *has not* done everything he could have; often he could have worked harder, studied harder, and tried harder. He may not know what constitutes his best academic effort because it has never been asked from him before. Here is where the fine line between academic success and failure often lies. The student-athlete suspects deep down that he has not given his 100 percent best effort. He may not admit it, but he is aware of it, and more likely than not, he secretly yearns to try harder. But risk and fear, those age-old emotions, inevitably creep into his psyche. Nobody enjoys failure, especially Division I–caliber athletes who are used to the sometimes phenomenal success of their athletic exploits. Putting forth one's best effort in a class and receiving a D or an F has a way of scything through the ego. It is much easier to go back to the dorm uttering pronouncements of disdain for school or hatred of an instructor than it is to walk into an academic adviser's office and say, "You know, I truly did my best and flunked. Can you help me?"

Living with failure is never easy, which is why coaches are fired and cash-paying fans and boosters grumble, stay home, and watch "Roseanne" when the victories do not mount. Student-athletes, through their years of athletic participation, have picked up on this credo: Winners are heroes; losers are bums. Therefore, by copping out and rationalizing, many athletes completely avoid the prospect of losing academically: They simply do not play the game.

First-Generation Students

The individual is always, at the very least, somewhat responsible for his plight, but as has been accentuated here, many other factors join to shape and give form to his existence. These environmental or external (both terms seem cold and hard, and they describe phenomena that often are) influences play an undeniable role in hindering the academic progress of student-athletes, especially low-income minority student-athletes. Although the individual's vast human potential should be able to surmount the obstacles of the environment, the challenge is anything but easy and is one from which many shy away. This is why one particularly problematic hurdle can be that of the first-generation college student. Second-, third-, and fourth-generation students approach higher education from a comfort zone, ripe with confidence and certainty. If a graduating high school senior knows that his grandfather and his father graduated from Yale, he may not harbor the slightest doubt that he will successfully follow in their footsteps.

The situation may be quite different for a black kid from Atlanta's Fulton High who is unaware of a single relative with a college degree. A first-generation college student from a disadvantaged background carries no assumption that he will graduate, and he has no related familial experiences to call on. College might not even have been a viable consideration until college recruiters came knocking, and even then, it may have been merely an afterthought. Of course, being a first-generation college student does not in itself mean certain failure, but in combination with the many other challenges awaiting the minority student-athlete, it can only intensify the struggle for success.

Related to the doubts of the first-generation college student, and mentioned earlier, is the belief that many black athletes need more and stronger academic role models. The devastating effect of the father's absence from the black home is a well-documented American tragedy; together with the shortage of appropriate academic-athlete role models, it goes far in explaining the academic difficulties experienced by many of today's black male Division I athletes. A seminar entitled "The Black Student Athlete: Models for Success," held during the annual meeting of the Congressional Black Caucus in 1987, focused on the need for appropriate academic modeling. Eric Floyd of the National Basketball Association and Lynn Swann, formerly with the National Football League's Pittsburgh Steelers, were invited to participate in the seminar because they, as black athletes, had graduated from Georgetown University and the University of Southern California, respectively. Floyd urged students to "use the sport, don't let it use you," and he added, "there's no one in front of the library saying it's off limits to athletes. If you don't want an education, you won't (get it)."[73] Swann, sounding less upbeat and probably more realistic, portrayed the current situation best when, speaking of himself and Floyd, he stated, "I wish that instead of being the role model, we were the rule, not the exception."

The View From the Ivory Tower: The Institution's Role in the Plight of the Student-Athlete

The American college is an intriguing institution. Loosely based on the classical university of the Middle Ages, today's center for higher learning must serve a clientele that demands preparation for unique career opportunities but that lacks the broad-based interdisciplinary background prerequisite to such specialization. The institution has become a catchall, a credential factory where an incredibly diverse student body matriculates for an even more incredible number of reasons. Today's universities are expected to be research centers, bastions of the liberal arts, vocational training facilities, publishing houses, hospitals, centers of advocacy, convention centers, cultural islands, profit makers, successful athletic competitors, and a score of other bizarre and contradictory things. In a pluralistic society, this may not necessarily be a negative state of affairs, but it certainly leads to confusion.

In the middle of this academic setting, jauntily swaggering through the mire, are collegiate athletic programs. Haughty in their current popularity, gloating over their financial significance, athletic departments have become an integral—albeit tainted—element of the academic community. Academicians roll their eyes and shake their heads over the antics of their campus brethren, pausing from their contempt only long enough to bask in the national limelight so often attracted by the athletic programs they despise. It is an interesting coexistence. The mixing of the athletic side with the academic side can truly yield a strange brew.

Into this rocky marriage, carting their suitcases full of well-documented strengths and weaknesses, come the student-athletes. Mere mortals that they are, avoiding their own snares and nooses would be accomplishment enough. But as in any adventure, additional troubles lurk around every corner. The institutions themselves are partly responsible: Their infighting, hypocrisy, and greed are the primary culprits. It is not enough that a student-athlete often enters college with skill deficiencies and an inadequate academic background. He must, in addition, play that poorly dealt hand with a partner who makes all the wrong moves at all the wrong times.

If the colleges and universities are the American think tanks that they claim to be, what dire consequences must surely await the populace! This is the conclusion one may draw if higher education's callous handling of the fragile lives of its student-athletes reflects its true abilities and nature. One hopes it does not, and, admittedly, the previous portrayal is laden with sarcasm. Still, higher education itself plays a primary role in the athletic-academic dilemma, and subtle and not-so-subtle actions and mind-sets of the American university should be reviewed and contemplated.

Colleges and universities have been able to publicly maintain the "academics first" credo for a long time. For this they deserve kudos because, first, it represents an expert con job and, second, the constant harping on the subject may have some administrators actually believing it is true. Of course, survival and financial stability are two major goals of many American universities, and a good number of institutions' actions are directed toward these two ends.

The current situation is not necessarily the fault of the institutions and their leaders. Society's support system for higher education and

America's admirably democratic passion for educating every citizen have resulted in most schools' relying heavily on state revenues and/or private donations. If tuition were the lone revenue source, schools would simply provide services for those enrolled, and institutional expenditures would fluctuate with supply and demand. However, this would result in an elitist system, with only those of wealth and leisure able to afford a tuition intended to cover all of the institution's costs. Any present-day institution that attempted to survive on tuition alone would wither and die.

Capitalism: The American Way

Financial realities are not the only obstacles for those yearning for an ideal state of academic purity. The true power brokers of colleges and universities, the regents and donors, are usually successful business people who are quite used to and comfortable with operating under the profit motive. In this context, it is only natural for a major university to function as a sort of quasi corporation, evolving with and reacting to the trends and movements of the marketplace that prove most profitable. If Benjamin Franklin's proposal that school boards and educational governing bodies should consist of sagacious and altruistic public servants holding life terms had been adopted, the current capitalistic approach to higher education might not have developed. But Franklin's school board idea went the way of his wild-turkey-as-the-national-bird idea and left America with a collegiate system in which the ISUs are barely distinguishable from the IBMs.

Modern collegiate athletics is, essentially, a monetary endeavor, and unfortunately, the student-athlete is often caught between the financial vanguard and the academic puritans. Educators, naturally, are quick to blame the evil monetary influences that "poison" so many facets of the university experience. This is a myopic viewpoint, though, for the educators' so-called reforms, homogeneous instructional methods, approaches to remediation, degree programs, double standards, and attitudes contribute as much as anything else to the problems of student-athletes, especially black student-athletes. However, the financial relationship between athletics and higher education is also at fault, and the deceptively strong bond between the two deserves consideration.

Greed in the Locker Room

College athletics and visions of monetary profits are hardly strangers. The transition of college sports from a mere extracurricular activity to a profitable endeavor occurred during the "Gilded Age" of the 1920s. This gradual process is probably best exemplified by the decline in the importance of the team captain or graduate manager and the rise to power of

the professional coach. Knute Rockne, perhaps more than any other figure, is the quintessential embodiment of this phenomenon. Rockne became an entertainment institution, and Notre Dame, a then typical and
relatively unknown midwestern Catholic college, was quick to capitalize
on the profits and publicity resulting from the altered focus.[1] College
athletics for profit has been the norm for large institutions ever since; the
only real changes have been the expanding scope of its financial structure
and inflation, which together have caused the money involved to reach
astronomical figures.

Before examining the actual revenue situation in Division I athletics,
one should note that this is an area of much debate. Many critics believe
that athletic programs never make money for their institutions, and they
are quick to point to athletic department deficits at such big-time schools
as Michigan, Maryland, and Wisconsin. Further, these same critics claim
that when athletic departments are profitable, it is the athletic departments (often private foundations) themselves that keep the money. Both
of these arguments are sound, but as in so many situations, reality may
be less important than how people perceive reality.

In any event, athletic programs' revenues, expenses, and (sometimes)
profits have skyrocketed over the last 3 decades. The annual budget for
a Division I football-playing school can be as much as $15 million, with
the football budget representing nearly half the total. Men's basketball,
while less expensive, still accounts for expenditures of at least $400,000.
A Division I school, statistically speaking, can, on the average, expect
revenues to exceed expenses by around $100,000, but this figure is very
misleading.[2] The NCAA, for all its talk of fair play and brotherhood, is
one of the best examples of the rich getting richer and the poor getting
poorer: The $100,000 "typical" profit is completely inaccurate. This is
because megaprograms like those at Notre Dame, Oklahoma, and Southern California realize huge profits, while the Indiana States, James Madi-
sons, and Northern Arizonas often operate in the red, possibly
scrounging money from the bookstore, campus vending machines, and
even health center earnings to keep athletic programs afloat. The reason
for this dichotomy is quite obvious. The high-profile programs in the
high-profile conferences receive more media exposure, win more championships, and parlay the resulting revenues into superior teams that
ensure the perpetuation of their exclusive club at the top. Once in a
while, a small Division I program can jump on this rapidly moving
merry-go-round (DePaul's basketball program is an example), but the
leap is treacherous, the odds are not good, and the wait is long.

Although the smaller Division I institutions, schools playing I-AA football in particular, may not be sharing in the revenue fallout, an examination of the NCAA budget figures does reveal an apparently rosy picture
for the overall economic health of big-time athletics. NCAA expenses
may have grown from $22,376,004 in 1981 to $69,476,470 in 1988, but

revenues saw an even more dramatic increase. The organization's 1981 revenue total was $23,331,263, resulting in a "surplus" (the NCAA's term) of $955,259. The year 1988, though, produced revenues of $82,808,606, and the so-called surplus had grown to the incredible sum of $13,332,136.[3] In 1990 total revenues reached the $92 million mark. The Chrysler Corporation should be so lucky! It does seem unusual for an amateur sports association to be reeling in millions of dollars in profits each year. Of course, the only thing amateur about NCAA sports is, supposedly, the athletes, and herein lies one of the rudimentary contradictions facing college athletics in general.

Television Revenue

Entertainment revenue of this magnitude can come from only one source: television. The national media coverage of NCAA athletics, both nectar and poison to the organization, has definitely influenced the infrastructure of the sports themselves. The growth of college sports on television has paralleled the growth of the NCAA. Walter Byers, the NCAA's first executive, was the organization's only full-time employee and occupied the rear corner of the Big Ten office when he took the job in 1951. When Byers retired in 1987, the NCAA had mushroomed into a bureaucracy of over 100 employees with a large office complex in Mission, Kansas. The organization is growing at an even faster rate now, with a recently opened state-of-the-art headquarters facility and an operating budget of $17.6 million.

NCAA television beginnings were just as innocent. In 1952, the initial year for televised college football, the National Broadcasting Company (NBC) paid $1.14 million for exclusive rights to the first NCAA football package. NBC held the rights until 1966, when they were nabbed by the American Broadcasting Corporation (ABC) for $7.8 million. The package and rights remained with ABC for 16 seasons, and the money and ratings soared. However, despite the increasingly healthy situation, there was grumbling by the larger and more successful schools that the NCAA monopoly was costing them money and that more revenue could be generated if they struck deals on their own. Therefore, in 1981, the 63-member College Football Association (the big-time powers excluding the Big 10 and PAC 10 conferences) signed a $100 million deal with NBC in blatant "defiance of NCAA control of the marketplace."[4] This same volatile year saw the University of Oklahoma and the University of Georgia file suit against the NCAA claiming price fixing, output restraints, and monopolizing. Both universities, seeking relief under the Sherman Antitrust Act, believed they could develop a more lucrative independent television package because of their immense regional followings.[5] Oklahoma University was even toying with the idea of pay television. The trend continued when, later in the same year, the NCAA membership voted to split its package deal between ABC and the Columbia Broadcasting System (CBS), and a supplemental package was worked out with the cable-based Turner Broadcasting System. It seemed as if the pot of gold was growing larger, and everyone anxiously awaited the court's rulings on the Oklahoma-Georgia suit.

On June 27, 1984, the greedy sportsmongers got their way. The Supreme Court, in a seven-to-two decision, found the NCAA television package in violation of the Sherman Antitrust Act. Like greased pigs at the county fair, the Oklahomas and the Bowling Greens scrambled and wallowed in the muck of TV-land, trying to secure the most lucrative deal. It seemed that every conference had some kind of package, and there was hardly a waking weekend moment when a television set could not be turned on to a game broadcast via the networks, cable, or syndication.

Something unexpected happened, though. The law of supply and demand intervened, and the first year saw total television revenue drop $15 million. This, of course, was due to a saturated market that made the "big games" no "big deal." Not only did the big-name schools suffer; the smaller members of Division I-AA, II, and III, who had at least received nominal revenues in the original NCAA packages, were now left with virtually no television revenues. It seemed that few media groups were champing at the bit to televise the likes of Austin Peay versus Eastern Kentucky. The next few years saw a continuing decline in television ratings and revenues. Some schools, like Oklahoma, for example, earned $200,000 less per televised game than they had originally. Perhaps the great financial wizards of the OU athletic department should have strolled across campus to the economics department before delving into the world of financial speculation.[6]

Fortunately for the big boys, a little annual roundball frenzy commonly referred to as the Final Four picked up some of the slack. So popular and hedonistic has this event become that in November of 1989, CBS Sports, Inc., agreed to pay the NCAA $1 billion for the rights to televise the tournament from 1991 through 1997. The enormity of this sum has had an immediate impact. Traditional conference affiliations that seemed etched in stone may fall by the wayside as schools scramble for league alternatives that may offer the chance to procure a larger chunk of this incredible sum of money. Even the sting of Notre Dame negotiating its own $38 million football package with NBC was assuaged by the NCAA's collective drool over the CBS deal.

Revenue From Nontraditional Sources

Still, much of the CBS loot will have to be earned on the court, and other avenues to raise athletic revenues have also been explored, especially by the smaller Division I programs that had been removed from the tele-

Men's NCAA Payoffs

Men's basketball tourney payoffs have risen dramatically during the last decade, and the CBS windfall will increase them even more.

	Payoff ($)	
Tournament stage	1980	1990
First round	81,594	286,500
Second round	81,594	573,000
Regional	203,986	859,500
Regional Finals	203,986	1,146,000
Final Four	326,378	1,432,500

Source: "Payout Estimated at $35.5 Million." *The NCAA News*, 28 March 1990, 1.

vised football economic pipeline. Some of the nontraditional alternatives were ingenious; others were ludicrous. They included endowments (University of Southern California secured endowments for 24 football starters' scholarships at $250,000 each); corporate sponsors (San Diego State grossed $1.2 million in sponsorships by allowing major companies to underwrite individual games); life insurance policies (Duke offers the Iron Dukes life insurance program, which lets people take out policies and name the Blue Devils as beneficiary, bringing a whole new meaning to the phrase "gone to the devil"); and even beer and cigarette taxes (an Oregon tax hike on beer and cigarettes to help support the state's Division I athletic programs was overwhelmingly defeated at the polls, although the state's voters did eventually approve legalized sports gambling).[7] Creative revenue alternatives will continue to be examined as the cost of competition increases and the taxpayers' revolt of the Reagan era continues.

Although an Iron Duke participant may sleep well at night dreaming of postmortem dunks and touchdowns, benefactors would prefer seeing a few of these events during their lifetimes. This brings up the point that the quickest and surest way to increase revenue is to win. Schools know this. *Everybody* knows this. It is the reason no one has ever heard of the University of Nebraska holding a raffle to raise money for athletics. Who needs to fiddle around with awarding Caribbean cruises when 76,000 loyal, donating maniacs file into your stadium every other Saturday? Of course, if the Cornhuskers went 0–10 for 3 years running, the stadium would probably be a trifle more empty. This is why the pressure is so intense—pressure to win, pressure to bring in the blue-chip athlete. When coaches say they *need* to go out and get a big man, they mean it. They need him to compete, they need him to win, they need him to make money for the institution, they need him to keep their jobs!

Relationship of Talent to Revenue

A single talented athlete can mean so much to an institution. It may be for all the wrong reasons, but one "impact" recruit can sometimes put a program over the hump and increase a school's notoriety and visibility. Sometimes an impact player can even lift a school out of relative obscurity. Patrick Ewing was just that kind of player.

West of the Appalachians, people rarely heard about Georgetown University, and they lost little sleep over the fact. Patrick Ewing changed all that. He and his coach, John Thompson, transformed the little-known Georgetown Hoyas into the New York Yankees of college basketball. "Hoya Paranoia" and "The Beast of the East" became easily recognized icons, while Thompson's staunch support of academics and his team's high-caliber play propelled Georgetown into the national spotlight.

Doug Flutie is another athlete who singlehandedly vaulted his team and school into prominence. The national perception of Boston College's Eagles, correct or incorrect, was that they epitomized college football mediocrity. Along came Flutie, though, and the Eagles began appearing on national telecasts as millions of viewers watched in anticipation of yet another Flutie miracle.

Economically, what did these two young men mean to their institutions? A Washington, DC, business journal projected Ewing's value to Georgetown University at $12 million, including "$4 million in additional revenue from attendance at games, $2.25 million for appearances in NCAA tournament games, and an estimated (some say conservatively) $3.4 million in additional alumni giving."[8] Flutie's worth to Boston College was reported to be in the same ballpark. These figures may have been somewhat fanciful and misleading, but it cannot be denied that ticket and television revenues, alumni giving, and freshman enrollment soared because of these schools' new national images.

An excellent example of the positive correlation between sports and finance is Southwest Missouri State University, where in 1980 the decision was made for the school to seek Division I status in athletics. The first 3 "limbo" years of probationary status saw the program flounder, especially the success of the basketball program—the primary motive for the Division I move in the first place. The year 1983, however, saw the hiring of Charlie Spoonhour, a successful junior college coach who was at that time serving as an assistant to head coach Moe Iba at Nebraska. Spoonhour, who was jocular and accessible from his first day, enjoyed tremendous success and became immensely popular. He built a respectable program that reached the quarterfinals of the National Invitation Tourney and earned four consecutive bids to the NCAA postseason tourney. Most notable, though, was the increase in attendance. The average attendance at home games soared from 4,000 in 1983 to 8,200 in 1989—a remarkable increase.

These accomplishments alone would have made the Spoonhour era notable, but they were paralleled by even more advancements in other areas. In 1983–84, Spoonhour's first season, monetary gifts to the university totaled $845,204, a modest sum for an institution with an enrollment of nearly 15,000. By 1987–88, however, the monetary gifts had surged forward to the sum of $3,662,067. This increase was matched by growth in total foundation assets from $1,315,388 to $5,763,627 during the same period. These years also saw enrollment increase from 14,552 to 17,006, and the sizes of the freshman classes increased by 39 percent. All this, amazingly, occurred at a time when many campuses nationwide were struggling to maintain the status quo in enrollment.[9]

Many hardworking people were responsible for the growth experienced by Southwest Missouri State University, but without Spoonhour and the publicity gained by his basketball program, the level of success would not have been so high. Spoonhour was the proverbial goose that laid the golden egg—several of them, in fact. Anyone viewing the Southwest Missouri situation honestly realized that the school's phenomenal growth had much to do with its quick-witted coach. What was Spoonhour's monetary worth to the university, to the community, or to the entire Ozarks region, for that matter? It is difficult to say, but an estimate in the $4 million to $5 million plus range is not outlandish. Of course, all of this is predicated on winning. As nice and funny as Charlie Spoonhour may be, a few 7-20 seasons or a string of humiliating losses to Valparaiso University might find the coach rudely ushered out of town by a gnarly band of modern-day Baldknobbers. Such is life in the fast lane of Division I athletics, where the only equation one needs to know is that victories equal dollars.

Maybe Southwest Missouri State's situation is an anomaly. Many argue that winning athletic programs do not result in increased giving to the academic sector of a university. Rick Telander, in his bitter critique of college football, *The Hundred Yard Lie*, cites studies and examples that would seem to substantiate this point. Notre Dame, for example, experienced an increase in academic donations during the lackluster Gerry Faust era, and Wichita State University's annual giving nearly doubled the year after that institution dropped football altogether.[10] These tangible arguments are hard to refute, and the actual amount of money realized from winning teams may often be overestimated. However, how many people would ever have heard of Notre Dame without football?

Why do so many students choose land grant institutions with the big-time atmosphere over state-supported regional schools? As nebulous as the actual monetary rewards may be, this notoriety and popularity with potential students are the intangibles that make athletics important to many boosters, regents, and administrators.

Recently, Sacred Heart University added the sports of football, lacrosse, and women's soccer as part of its "5-year strategic plan." Anthony J. Cernera, president of the school, said, "This news is exciting to all of us at Sacred Heart University. We are sure it will enhance the quality of student life and present an additional reason for alumni support."[11] Maybe Dr. Cernera is thinking along the same lines as a few Notre Dame administrators of nearly 75 years ago.

The Universities' Unclear Academic Expectations for Athletes

The greed of institutions and their athletic departments is obviously problematic, but it is not the sole culprit. The academic practices and philosophies of many universities hardly help the situation. Add the often confusing attitudes of some academicians, and no one could blame a student-athlete for crying out the old Steeler's Wheel line, "Clowns to the left of me, jokers to the right, here I am, stuck in the middle with you."

Cries for Reform

Educational reform has swept the country like a wind-blown prairie brushfire. Everybody wants to reform something. Reform this, reform that, sometimes reform reforms. Missouri's governor, John Ashcroft, wanted to reform the public schools of his state by adding 60 days to the school calendar. Of course, there was no mention of how this reform would be financed, nor did anyone seem to question how simply doing more of the same thing constituted reform. Apparently, these minor details did not matter. The governor had proposed a reform, by golly, and he could now call himself the Education Governor.

Higher education has also heard the plaintive cries for reform, and the political and public pressure to improve has resulted in tougher entrance standards, more stringent degree requirements, and in some instances, exit testing. Many of these changes may have been necessary, and most successful students will probably make the proper adjustments. Unfortunately, though, the implementation of these tougher academic expectations is occurring simultaneously with an increase in pressure to build and maintain a financially successful (winning) athletic program. This poses some intriguing problems for coaches and athletic directors. To win in the two major revenue sports, many coaches believe they must recruit athletes who eat, sleep, and breathe basketball or football. This myopic commitment to a sport is often found in low-income communities, where athletic excellence may be perceived as the only avenue to fame and fortune. Many of the athletes who subscribe to this single-minded devotion—a devotion that does reap benefits on the field and the court—are academically unprepared blacks. These young men are then placed in a scholastic environment where there is less and less flexibility and tolerance.

Athletic directors, coaches, and athletic academic advisers are cognizant of this apparent catch-22. They feel they are damned if they do and damned if they don't, and there are no quick and easy solutions.

Dear Athletic Director

I wrote the following letter and sent it to our athletic department personnel in hopes of shedding light on the dilemma academically unprepared black students face in institutions of higher learning. The first names and initials of the players mentioned are all fictitious.

Dear (   ),

I believe the Southwest Missouri State basketball program is approaching a catch-22 regarding academic achievement and athletic success. The program, attempting to compete successfully at the Division I level, is forced to recruit junior college players with marginal scholastic abilities. The university, however, is simultaneously upgrading its academic requirements and making it increasingly difficult for marginal students to advance in a degree program. This situation is even more ironic when one considers that the university is crediting much of its prestige and growth to the success of the basketball program. I strongly believe that this problem demands further attention. Consider the following:

1. Students such as Gary G., John J., Marty M., Chris C., and Don D. do not possess the necessary academic skills (writing, reading, mathematics) to graduate from the university without an immense amount of help. A part-time academic adviser working within the framework of the university's piecemeal remediation program cannot adequately meet the needs of these students. Charlie C. is a prime example. Charlie has run into a major roadblock with his 6 hours of required _____ course work. I do not have the time nor resources to adequately supervise or participate in the type of tutorial program that would ensure Charlie's success. I hope things will work out for him.

(Cont.)

I can currently concentrate heavily on one student at a time (e.g., Sam S.) while monitoring the academic progress, attendance, and registration of the other players. Unfortunately, we probably have five or six other players (Marty M., John J., Gary G., Charlie C., Olin O., and possibly William W.) needing the same amount of attention. Our recruits for next season may only add to this predicament.

2. What will happen if a number of our players fail to graduate? I think some members of the university community will question whether the players are being exploited by the university. Obviously, this would not enhance the reputation of the program or the university. I believe it is the ethical responsibility of the university to provide adequate academic support for student-athletes, whose accomplishments mean so much to the university.

3. The university is currently reviewing its inadequate remediation program. I served on the Remediation Task Force that made recommendations for the areas of remediation and academic support. Coach _____ has a copy of the proposal, but the financing and implementation of the program will take years. Our needs are immediate. If we fail to take action, I fear many of our players will not graduate.

We have many pluses! We have *great kids*, concerned coaches, and a supportive faculty, and I am willing to work my butt off. However, we need a more systematic approach to meeting our players' academic needs.

I realize that players compound their scholastic difficulties by skipping class and not studying, but the university is still *morally obligated* to offer the appropriate academic support. After all, a student-athlete reading at the fourth- or fifth-grade level can go to class until the moon turns blue, but attendance alone will not ensure that he successfully comprehends a college textbook.

Much to the credit of our athletic director and coaches, this letter received a positive response. We increased our efforts for these marginal students, and two of the players mentioned went on to graduate.

Difficulty of Access to Degree Programs

Nationally the problem still exists, and it is further illustrated by difficulties with the recruitment and retention of minority future teachers. Thousands of black, Hispanic, American Indian, and other minority students have been denied entrance to teacher education programs because they have not passed recently legislated state-required standardized tests.[12] In fact, "between 1976 and 1983, the percentage of bachelor's degrees in education awarded to blacks decreased 52 percent, and with new competency tests for licensure and certification of teachers, the percentage of minority teachers may become even less."[13] This statement draws attention to the plight of many minority students who, once admitted to the general education curriculum of an institution, find many degree programs inaccessible because they cannot meet grade point average or standardized test score requirements—requirements that often call for above average performance. Students falling into this category drift in an academic no-man's-land, choosing majors solely on the basis of access. Naturally, under the pressure of academic snobbery, many of the more accessible departments will feel it necessary to raise their own standards to avoid projecting the image of a scholastic landfill. One professor remarked about his university, "The entire situation is absurd. Students can be admitted, stay in school and off probation, and be accepted in hardly any degree programs. And these are students with C averages." Obviously, the academically struggling athlete is a prime candidate for this illogical scenario.

The Factory Model of Education

The factory model of education has sturdy historical roots. English language instruction is as responsible for it as anything else. During the 19th century, the powerful influences of nationalism and capitalism molded a public school system whose mission was to Americanize a vast immigrant population and create a viable work force.[14] Industrialization was the underlying motive, and supplying the mills and factories with adequate labor became essential to the nation's economic needs. Today's economy, however, is changing, and the former product-oriented, homogeneous approach to schooling is no longer appropriate. Institutions of higher education, particularly state-supported regional institutions, constantly face the dilemma of educating a heterogeneous student body with means designed for a homogeneous population. Student-athletes, with their wide range of socioeconomic backgrounds, their dual purpose in attending college, and the unusual demands on their time and energy, are a group often slighted by educational strategies designed for the traditional college student.[15] This discrepancy has been recognized by many educators, and remedial classes or developmental programs have been initiated on many campuses to help students and, most important to the institutions' financial well-being, to increase student retention. Most such programs are legitimate and well-meaning, but even these are sometimes abused by people who perceive them as academic havens for struggling student-athletes.

The Georgia Fiasco

On the other hand, some developmental programs are bogus from the start. A most peculiar example of this arose in the quaint college town of Athens, Georgia.

Jan Kemp had taught in the remedial studies department at the University of Georgia for years before she was dismissed from her appointment. In 1983, Kemp filed suit against the university, claiming she was fired because she had protested giving passing grades to University of Georgia athletes who had flunked developmental studies courses. Technically, the lawsuit involved freedom of speech—Kemp's lawyer maintained she was fired for her criticism of the preferential treatment of athletes—but it was the university's developmental studies program and athletic department that were actually on trial.[16] The University of Georgia's developmental studies program was "designed to make a university education available to students from disadvantaged backgrounds."[17] Athletes made up 17 percent of the program's enrollment, and the basic skills courses they took did not count toward any degree programs. The conflict surfaced when an academic affairs administrator, who had instructed Kemp to change F's to incompletes, allegedly queried, "Who do you think is more important to the University, you or a very prominent basketball player?"[18]

The details of the events leading to Kemp's dismissal remained muddled throughout the trial, but the attitude and arrogance of the athletic department eventually decided the verdict. At one point, a secretly made tape recording of a meeting of school officials was played as evidence. It contained the voice of Le Roy Ervin, the academic affairs administrator who had challenged Kemp. On tape, Ervin explained the athlete's role at the University of Georgia:

> I know for a fact that these kids would not be here if it were not for their utility to the institution. There is no real academic reason for their being here other than to be utilized to produce income. They are used as a kind of raw material in the production of some goods to be sold . . . [and they get to be sold . . .] and they get nothing in return.[19]

As shocking as this admittance of exploitation must have been, the attorney representing the University of Georgia, Hale Almand, was not to be outdone when he described the athletic program in this manner:

> We may not make a university student out of an athlete. But if we can teach him to read and write, maybe he can work at the post office rather than as a garbage man when he gets through with his athletic career.[20]

Whether Almand's statement was degrading, racist, stupid, or all three, it was met with widespread scorn and outrage, and the jury promptly socked the university by awarding Kemp $2.5 million in damages.

The entire legal proceeding was a highly publicized three-ring circus. Kemp divorced, attempted suicide, and found God via religious fundamentalism. The university stumbled and stammered, and everything its representatives said or did seemed to have a certain foot-in-mouth ineptness. Although Kemp won and the battle was heated and dirty, she, amazingly enough, remained a devout Bulldog fan through and through, even to the point of worrying about whether the trial would affect her chances of getting season tickets for the next football season.[21]

Kemp's University of Georgia fiasco may be somewhat out of the ordinary, but the fact remains that many Division I institutions take advantage of bogus course offerings to ensure the eligibility of academically deficient student-athletes. Not all of these slippery academic avenues are necessarily illegal, either. Minisemester classes and special intersession offerings are usually available to all students, and the fact that many athletes load up on such classes only shows that they have enough awareness to seize the opportunities that will net them the 24 credit hours necessary for annual eligibility. Of course, the NCAA is all too cognizant of the stereotypical, jock-oriented, basket weaving–type scheduling, and for this reason, current regulations mandate that a participating student-athlete must demonstrate progress toward a degree. The problem here is enforcement, as determining what actually constitutes progress toward a degree is an imprecise business at best. Therefore, schools have a certain latitude, and remedial or developmental programs have a nice "gee,-let's-help-these-kids" sound to them and an incredible knack for producing the desired grade results. Unfortunately, as in the Georgia case, the developmental/remedial programs often fail the students and, in essence, fail the university. As one academically serious junior college basketball recruit asked me, "You're not going to stick me in any of those RIF ["Reading is Fundamental"] classes, are you?"

"What's Your Major?"

As NCAA class scheduling requirements have tightened, and as graduation rates have become a litmus test for an athletic department's academic integrity, a strange new academic major has appeared at some Division I institutions. This is the general studies degree, or the social science degree, or the social science general degree, or whatever creative and scholarly sounding moniker may spring from an academic affairs office's imagination. Such degree programs have, in some instances, been invented specifically for athletes, and they are becoming more and more prevalent as schools are being held increasingly accountable for the graduation rates of their athletes. The programs vary from school to school, but they are basically interdisciplinary, generalist programs with a healthy amount of flexibility. Kansas State University, which has boasted about its athletes' high graduation rate, has a social science degree program where, reportedly, many different classes can be credited to the athlete's degree program. While this "stone soup" approach to class scheduling enables an athlete to walk to the podium and receive a diploma, it is hard to imagine what skills he is actually gaining. Harry Edwards accurately assesses the problems of phony degree programs and related classes:

> Under circumstances where the grades obtained in many of the courses taken by student athletes are deficient or "automatic" or "fixed" rather than earned, there is little wonder that so many black scholarship athletes manage to go through four years of college enrollment virtually unscathed by education. Not surprisingly either, studies show that as many as 65–75 percent of those black student athletes awarded collegiate athletic scholarships may never graduate from college (as opposed to 30–35 percent of white student athletes). Of the 25–35 percent who do eventually graduate from the schools they play for, an estimated 60–65 percent of them graduate either with physical education degrees or in Mickey Mouse jock majors specifically created for athletes and generally held in low repute (as compared to 33 percent of white student athletes in such majors).[22]

Schools without phony majors are quite aware of the schools that have them, and this awareness resulted in an interesting rules battle at the 1988 NCAA Convention held in Nashville, Tennessee. A proposal from the NCAA Presidents Commission would have strengthened regulations regarding satisfactory progress. The proposal stated:

> The student-athlete must achieve the following accumulative minimum grade-point average (based on a maximum of 4.000) at the certifying institution to fulfill the "satisfactory completion" requirement of this provision: (1) 1.600 after the completion of the first season of competition; (2) 1.800 after the completion of the second season of competition; and (3) 2.000 after the completion of the third season of competition and subsequent seasons of competition.[23]

The proposal, which sounds logical enough, was initially passed by the assembly. However, after much discussion and heated debate, the assembly voted to reconsider the proposal and tabled it. It seems that some schools figured out that the new rule would create an advantage for schools with phony degree programs, and they argued that it would be inherently unfair for a player studying aeronautical engineering to be denied eligibility for a 1.9 grade point average while a player majoring in general studies and accumulating a 2.1 GPA was allowed to compete. The dispute created some unusual alliances on both sides of the issue, and the proposal has yet to pass.

General studies degree programs are not necessarily evil. It is the motivation behind them and the message they communicate that are unfortunate. They exist, sometimes, to ensure eligibility for student-athletes, and they hardly impart an attitude that academic concerns are at least as significant as athletics. True, some "general studies" may improve the lives of student-athletes dramatically, but their mere existence is an institutional admittance that a player's economic utility supersedes his academic needs and that no other viable alternatives can be found or constructed.

"The Absent-Minded Professor"

Although the institutional structure of a university may be detrimental to the academic growth of student-athletes, the prevailing attitudes of many administrators and faculty members do little to improve the situation. This is in part because higher education professionals generally feel that they are underpaid and receive little respect. Many have toiled for years in graduate school, and they have quite often chosen their career routes with lofty and idealistic notions of world and societal improvement. It irks them that "lesser educated" salesmen and businessmen often quadruple their salaries, and they realize that professorial types are generally held in low esteem by the economic-power elite. The professors often find a coping mechanism in rationalization, reveling in their own intellectual abilities or perceiving themselves as the last guardians of the academic bastion. This is fine and dandy until something cracks the walls of their ivory towers, and nothing cracks more devastatingly than ill-prepared student-athletes lounging in their classrooms, present in school only to entertain the businessmen-boosters, whose respect for the academic profession is so elusive.

Stereotyping and Pigeonholing

Obviously, multitudes of college professors do not fit this portrayal, but those who do refuse to see any value in athletic participation. These professors will not pragmatically accept the relationship between college athletics and the modern university. Instead, they perceive academically ill-prepared athletes as a menace to their mission and an insult to their profession. They did not study for 10 years to teach remedial reading. Dealing with student-athletes who are often unmotivated and unskilled only erodes the quality time they could be spending with more deserving students. English teachers are the best (or worst) example. Often endowed with a pompous, holier-than-thou attitude, many trained in the letters hold in total disdain those who most need their help. Stated Jan Kemp about this very situation:

> There are so many professors in this nation—English professors are the world's worst—who say, "We can't do anything with these [students] who are so deficient. We've got to accept only those who already have skill and talent." Well, that's blatant bigotry. You know what they're afraid of? They're afraid that if we teach minorities the power and force of the English language, that they'll have to listen to it in the boardroom.[24]

Kemp should have added that making the assumption that all students are capable of writing would mean acknowledging that one's own abilities might not be quite so unusual as one might have thought.

Whether or not anyone wants to admit it, Kemp's comments, applied to faculties in general, are true. This brings up the important point of pseudoliberalism. The very professors who despise college athletics are many times the same people who voice support for liberal issues and sympathy with the plight of the underprivileged. Yet, when faced with examples of their own causes in a classroom, they become defensive at the thought that their jobs have been compromised by the ugly troll they know as college athletics. Certainly, many faculty members have a right to be outraged at athletic programs' misappropriation of funds and the exploitation of student-athletes, but resenting the athlete is unfair and, more often than not, due to laziness and ego rather than staunch philosophical reasoning.

Situations like this one are most unfortunate, especially when studies show that the success of black college students is positively influenced by productive student-faculty interactions.[25] Undeniably, many student-athletes have failed academically because of their own self-defeating behaviors and attitudes,[26] but the conduct of professors should not be guided by stereotypes about student-athletes. Negative stereotypes perpetuate hypocritical attitudes and actions, and negative stereotypes are as common on today's campus as they are at the local truck stop. All student-athletes have to battle the dumb jock stereotype. Professors who have been "burned" by unmotivated or unskilled athletes often assume an athlete will be negligent in pursuing academic goals. This is regrettable: Many student-athletes are decent kids who want to succeed academically and do. Unfortunately, as U.S. Representative Thomas Luken (Republican, Ohio) has stated, that decent kid image is

---

Thanks for the Help, Prof!

A perfect illustration of the pseudoliberal attitude occurred at my institution, Southwest Missouri State University. A player from a predominantly black southern city needed only two courses to graduate with a Bachelor of Science degree in a specific major. Unfortunately for him, the two courses were in an area in which he struggled because of language and environmental factors. The young man was no Rhodes scholar, but he had a heart of gold and had approached every class with diligence and maximum effort. He had been active in community service, and his primary goal was to work with disadvantaged youth at a YMCA or a boys' club. He desperately needed his degree to acquire the credentials for such a responsible position.

I liked the young man immensely, and I was well aware of his trepidation about enrolling in the two courses. Knowing how far he had progressed since transferring from a junior college, and knowing about his positive impact on the entire community, I phoned the appropriate department head to inquire if the student might be placed with an instructor who would not mind spending some extra time to help him out.

The department head, at his present position for less than a year and typefying the "intellectual liberal" persona, responded with indignation. He declared that at his former institution, an Atlantic Coast Conference powerhouse, it was common knowledge that "those kinds of students don't get degrees." His change of institutions evidently had not altered his opinion, because he stated that he would do nothing to compromise his department's standards. He claimed that regardless of whose class the student enrolled in, he would personally make sure the young man was working at the appropriate "college level" before receiving a passing mark. I was shocked and disappointed at the defensiveness and vehemence of the department head's attitude.

---

not the stereotype of the jock, the dumb hulk of a brainless athlete who needs protection from the demands of a college education, but the stereotype is just a way of blaming the victim for the treatment he gets. We have to remember that—in every field—college athletes are often among the best. We have to start thinking of college athletes as having the potential of a Sen. Bill Bradley, who played basketball in college; a Rep. Jack Kemp, who played football; or a Gov. Mario Cuomo, who played baseball.[27]

Representative Luken's point would be well taken but for the fact that all three of his exemplars are white, and it is the black student-athlete who must contend with the most rigid stereotypical images. In fact, "black student-athletes from the outset have the proverbial 'three strikes' against them."[28] First, and obviously, black student-athletes encounter the "dumb jock" stereotype faced by all student-athletes, regardless of race. And black students are burdened with other negative beliefs. A particularly damaging one is the myth of innate black athletic superiority; it reinforces the notion that black athletes don't care about school, and it fosters a perception of blacks as animals or mere combatants. Even more regrettable is the blatant racist stereotype of the " 'dumb Negro' condemned by racial heritage to intellectual inferiority."[29] All three of these stereotypes represent difficult hurdles, and there is not a black student-athlete in the country who is unaware of their existence.

Unrealistic Expectations

Along with the stereotyping and pigeonholing of minority players, the intercollegiate athletic system has created unrealistic institutional pressures for all student-athletes. The players are expected to be full-time athletes and full-time students, and they encounter the additional intensified pressures of winning and maintaining average or above-average scholastic records. Grade inflation has made "C-minus student" a less-than-desirable label, and the institutional demand for the intellectual athlete is often unyielding and unjust. As Chancellor Charles Young of UCLA stated regarding the institutional pressures on athletes, "Students should not be required to spend 40 hours a week practicing and competing without any real break. That simply has resulted in having only the very most qualified students who are also athletes being able to graduate on time."[30]

James Rhatigan quipped about Division I basketball players:

No other students are required to miss 15–20 percent of their classes to receive their scholarships, grants, or loans. . . . For schools in post-season competition, the percentage of required absences on class days would approach 30 percent in the January-February-March period.[31]

The NCAA is currently haggling over practice and schedule limitations, but, regardless of the outcome, the time demands on student-athletes will remain outrageous.

The Athletic Department: Who Are These Guys, Anyway?

Complicating the already gnarled mess of institutional attitudes, practices, and pressures on the student-athlete are the adversarial relationships between academic faculties and athletic departments. Faculties sometimes view athletic department members as misguided clods intent on dehumanizing the academic environment and undermining everything intellectual. Athletic department personnel, on the other hand, often see faculty members as lazy, overpaid hypocrites who put in few hours of actual work and indulge their penchant for griping and being unrealistic. Both groups are probably right on some counts and wrong on others, the problem being that their respective missions, goals, and rationales for existence are like skew lines in space. Unfortunately, the athletes often get caught in the resulting disarray.

Athletic departments are sometimes quick to blame the disadvantaged educational backgrounds of many student-athletes for their array of academic problems. A few coaches and athletic administrators have even gone so far as to vow that their athletes are "owed an education," and they blame faculties for not doing enough to ensure the athletes' academic success. While both beliefs have a degree of truth in them, athletic department personnel all too often fail to see their own role in detracting student-athletes from educational pursuits. The very posture of athletic programs is responsible for this; the nature of their existence and the paradigm from which they operate create an environment that could hardly be perceived as conducive to scholarship. In fact, the athletic department's isolated status, recruiting practices, emphasis on winning, and attitudes in general all serve to hinder the academic pursuits of student-athletes.

For many years, coaching positions were filled by members of the physical education faculty. By no means did this state of affairs ensure complete academic integrity, but it was probably superior to the present situation, where most coaches in the revenue-producing sports have no academic obligations whatsoever. Obviously, this situation is due to the increased financial pressures on athletic programs. An athletic director cannot afford—literally—to hire a coach who will have to devote significant time to classroom duties.

There is nothing inherently wrong with employing coaches who reside outside the academic mainstream. The professorial ranks have no monopoly on ethics or knowledge, and there is no reason to believe that a nonacademic person cannot promote and support his players' academic endeavors. Regrettably, though, athletic departments have become increasingly isolated from the academic side of the university. Although the effect of this isolation may be more perception than tangible outcome, it definitely creates a sense of difference that may confuse the student-athletes and undermine the working relationship between the athletic departments and their academic counterparts. Again, Representative Luken addresses the issue:

> Americans who haven't seen it firsthand generally don't realize
> the extent to which big-money sports is distorting campus life

for student athletes. First of all, big-time athletics is not just another department of the university, like physics or philosophy or anthropology. The athletic department is often a separate corporation, with its own budget and administrative structure. Moreover, it recruits "talent" quite apart from the normal admissions procedure of the university.[32]

The separation of the athletic and the academic breeds mistrust and suspicion, especially when budgetary questions arise. Given this rift, creating the type of environment necessary to nurture the fledgling academic skills of struggling student-athletes is a difficult task.

Athletics not only quarantines student-athletes from the university mainstream, it also creates a logistic nightmare because of the ever-increasing length of the seasons. Football has gone from 10 games to 11, and some coaches and athletic administrators are advocating the inclusion of a 12th game. Basketball seasons have also taken on some eternal attributes. Seasons begin in early to mid-November with exhibition games and media-oriented events like the preseason National Invitation Tournament (NIT), and they do not end until the springtime culmination of March Madness. The reason behind the lengthy seasons is clearly and simply increased revenue. The idea is to milk the product (the student-athlete) for all he is worth.

Some people have recommended shortening sports practice periods, but it is not necessarily the practices that are problematic. Game travel and road trips interfere with regular class attendance. This interference is particularly acute in basketball, where scheduling has gotten completely out of hand. Most teams have played 30 or so games before the NCAA postseason tourney even begins, and many of the games are transcontinental affairs scheduled specifically for television. At the 1990 NCAA convention, members voted to reduce the basketball season by 3 games. However, so loud has the squawking been about lost revenue that the 3-game reduction may eventually be in jeopardy. Other alternatives to the present scheduling methods have been presented. Ladell Anderson, former head men's basketball coach at Brigham Young University, proposed one of the more novel, if controversial, ideas. Anderson, noting the conflicts with fall term finals, football bowl games, and Christmas breaks, suggested that the college basketball season begin after Christmas and climax in mid-April.[33] Although Anderson's proposal would break with tradition, it clearly has some merit. Sooner or later, the NCAA will have to realistically come to grips with a current scheduling system that exhibits all the careful planning of a runaway train.

Not only does the structure of intercollegiate sports chip away at a student-athlete's academic foundation, but also, in many instances, the prevailing attitudes of those involved in athletics contradict the ideals of higher education. Some coaches and athletic administrators demonstrate an almost antiintellectual attitude. This is, in itself, not unusual: The United States in general views intellectualism with a disdainful eye. College sports, however, are presumably still part of the college environment. While coaches should not forgo their lunches with insurance representatives and the like to dine with foreign language professors, they should at least adorn themselves with some trappings of the academic environment.

Some coaches and athletic administrators hold up the intellectual end quite admirably. Dean Smith, the University of North Carolina coach, is said to read Kierkegaard, and Paul Westhead, former coach at Loyola Marymount, reportedly taught in the school's English department. These examples are outside the norm, however, and the dialogue of some coaches may never transcend the most cherished topic of all, recruiting.

The Room of Schemes

Nothing may be more absurd than the recruitment of student-athletes. Consider North Carolina State University's "Room of Dreams," where basketball recruits would sit in isolation and view an audiovisual production depicting them as future collegiate stars. Consider the jet planes, limousines, phone calls from governors, college coed recruiting groups, recruiting films, and daily phone calls and notes that currently characterize college recruiting. If big-spending boosters want to know where their donated dollars go, this is it: the hardware and travel that make up recruiting.

Recruiting is not necessarily evil. If grown adults want to spend their time with 17-year-olds wooing and fawning, let them. The trouble arises, though, when recruiting becomes an end in itself. This happens when athletic programs, the coaches in particular, lose touch with reality—or, in other words, forget that they are part of an educational institution. The isolation of athletic departments contributes to this, and the inordinate pressure to win only exacerbates the problem.

Demoting Role of Academics

When the approach to recruiting is warped, academics are merely a hurdle to be hurdled or a puzzle to be solved. Consider the example of Lovelace Redmond. Lovelace, originally from Milwaukee, where he prepped at Washington High School, spent his freshman and sophomore years at Wyoming's Laramie Junior College. Lovelace was no Alonzo Mourning, but he was a good enough jumper and 3-point shooter that he was contacted by representatives from over 20 Division I schools. According to Lovelace, only two schools, Iowa State University and Southwest Missouri State University (which he eventually attended), even discussed his academic obligations, and one Division I school told him to forget about academics because they could provide him with all the credit hours he might need at a nearby junior college. This school must have meant it, too, because they reportedly had procured 24 hours of academic credit for another junior college transfer during the previous summer.

Herein lies the problem of recruiting. With all the hype surrounding the recruitment of an outstanding athlete, academics—hardly a glamorous topic—are often left out of the picture. Assuredly, many schools do stress scholarship (North Carolina reportedly sends out academic questionnaires to prospective student-athletes), but an equal number of programs avoid the issue altogether or, worse, as in Redmond's case, they downplay it. The implied message becomes loud and clear. Ball is the priority, and academics are a mere nuisance to be dealt with. This message may not be intentional, but the recruited athlete infers it. It then molds and shapes his attitude toward his upcoming academic work. Perhaps Charlie Vincent of the *Detroit Free Press* put recruiting into perspective when he wrote, "There was a time when athletics fit nicely into the framework of the university. Now, we have allowed it, in a lot of ways, to overshadow the purpose of the schools. It is now—at some of our nation's most prestigious institutions—show biz."[34]

Playing Up the "Quick Fix" Attitude

Show biz or not, the recruiting battles have done more than relegate academic concerns to the mental back burners of recruits. At their very worst, recruiting efforts portray for young, impressionable recruits a world where the "quick fix" is feasible and where the unethical shortcut will suffice. Cheating is the culprit here. If a player's services can be bought or obtained through unethical conduct, why can't grades? Also, a recruit who has been involved in a blatantly illegal situation must assume that the other actors in the scenario—coaches, boosters, administrators, whoever—will just as effectively and sneakily keep him out of academic purgatory. Outrageous cheating is probably not as widespread as some would imply, but its mere existence—however prevalent—guarantees that many student-athletes will assume that the flashy, gold-plated approach to life is quicker, easier, and more successful than a path where hard work and ethical values take precedence.

It is important at this point to recognize a fundamental difference between men's and women's athletics. As was stated in chapter 2, female athletes perform very well academically. The findings from the Colorado State study (1970–80), the Division I study (1986), the National Study of

Intercollegiate Athletics (1987–88), and the NCAA Academic Reporting Compilation (1989) all reiterate the fact that female student-athletes outperform their male counterparts in the classroom. Also, a simple scan of the print media would lead one to conclude that women's intercollegiate athletic competition has been spared the corruption so prevalent on the men's side. There are very logical explanations for these phenomena. First, intense pressure on women's athletic programs has been virtually nonexistent. In spite of Title IX and the increased resources allocated to women's programs, the pressures to win are lacking. This is due to the prevailing perception that women's sports are not and never will be revenue producers. There are occasional exceptions—the highly successful University of Texas women's basketball program, for instance—but overall, few campus administrators see women's athletics as having the potential to fatten university coffers.

A second reason for the apparent purity of women's athletics can be traced to the high school origins of girls' competition. This might be called the Un-Macho Factor. Most boys, regardless of academic or social inclinations, crave the notoriety of athletic participation. Strength, virility, and success are all self-perceptions that males have derived from successful sports competition. Girls' competition, in contrast, has historically been more comparable to participation in the glee club or the safety council, and it has lacked the high-powered social ramifications of membership in the cheerleading squad. Without the magnetizing positive feedback surrounding boys' athletics, there was nothing to lure marginal or disenfranchised female students into competition. This is changing, though. The acceptance and increasing popularity of girls' team sports is making participation more attractive. If women's intercollegiate programs become lucrative, they will undoubtedly begin facing many of the same perils as the men's.

Role of Junior Colleges

The negative attitudes and modeling of shady recruiting practices are often parlayed with the unscrupulous exploitation of junior colleges and their athletes. Nothing better exemplifies the seedy side of this combination than the modern-day slave auction known as basketball's JUCO Jamboree. Sponsored by recruiting services, businesses that specialize in providing information to coaching staffs, and held at the gymnasiums of various 4-year institutions, the JUCO Jamboree brings in from 12 to 20 junior college teams to play abbreviated games for hordes of talent-evaluating college coaches. The spectacle of throngs of mostly white coaches rating, judging, and grading the typically black athletes like stock at a county fair is demeaning at best and vulgar at worst. Certainly, a JUCO Jamboree gives a player the opportunity to impress a coach and gain a scholarship. But to a casual observer, the entire scene reeks of exploitation.

The Slave Trade

Harry Edwards, in his article "The Black Dumb Jock," delivered this indictment of the relationship between the Division I establishment and junior colleges:

> Many of these young men [black athletes] eventually end up in what is called, appropriately enough, the "slave trade"—a nationwide phenomenon involving independent scouts (some would call them flesh peddlers) who, for a fee (usually paid by a four-year college) searches [sic] out talented but academically high-risk athletes and places [sic] them in an accommodating junior college where their athletic skills are further honed through participation in sports of the junior college while they accumulate grades sufficient to permit them to transfer to the sponsoring four-year school.[a]

Note. [a]Harry Edwards, "The Black Dumb Jock," The College Board Review, Spring 1984, 9.

The opportunities and abuses of the JUCO Jamboree mirror the junior college athletic experience in general. Junior colleges may very well provide valuable chances for young men who have not developed to their fullest academic or athletic potential, but they may also be the settings for the worst types of abuse. The fact that Bobby Knight's highly respected Indiana program featured two prominent junior college transfers in winning the 1987 NCAA Championship seemingly vindicated the JUCO system and helped remove the academic tarnish that had stained many JUCO athletes' reputations. No longer taboo, the recruitment of "jukes" intensified and became more widespread. Proposition 48, the NCAA rule that bases freshman eligibility on standardized test scores, and its plethora of "nonqualifiers" only increased the use of the junior college system. In theory, there is nothing remotely wrong with a student-athlete's attending a junior college where he may receive more individualized help in both academics and athletics. It is bridging the theory-to-practice gap that is often difficult.

Forms of JUCO abuse or "legal cheating" are among the most clever and least publicized acts that college recruiters pull from their dirty bag of tricks. Consider the following amazing-but-true story. A national NCAA

Division II basketball powerhouse recruited a talented nonqualifier under the pretense that he would play at the school his freshman season, transfer to a nearby junior college for his sophomore year, and then be eligible to move on to a more attractive Division I setting. The player accepted the offer, signed a letter of intent with the Division II school, and spent his freshman season excelling on the hardwoods but floundering off the court. This was just the scenario the team's coaches had envisioned, and his academic floundering was allowed to continue for the entire season. At the end of the spring semester, the player had earned few academic credit hours. He blissfully transferred to the junior college, where he was essentially traded—a common practice—for another player. The transferred player assumed he was on his way toward Division I. But at the end of his junior college sophomore season, he had nowhere near the required credit hours to graduate from that school and was thus ineligible for Division I competition. As you may have guessed, the player ended up back at his original Division II school, where a creampuff schedule during his junior year would ensure athletic eligibility for his senior season.

Junior college shenanigans such as these are not unusual, and they probably represent one of the most hideous *and* prevalent modes of academic-athletic fraud. Inarguably, many junior colleges and their athletic programs are centers of integrity,[35] but the relationship between JUCO coaches and 4-year coaches is blood-brother thick: Its weblike network can harbor an amazing amount of intrigue and manipulation.

Pressure to Win

If the recruiting practices of athletic programs and the questionable use of junior colleges are responsible for undermining the academic integrity of players and programs alike, they have become so because coaches are under intense pressure from administrators and alumni to produce victories. These pressures, combined with the tremendous monetary and material rewards available to successful Division I coaches, motivate some in the business to use any means necessary to secure the skilled athlete. Bobby Knight and Dean Smith may be insightful motivators and extraordinary tacticians, but without the Isiah Thomases and Michael Jordans, their national titles would have been elusive at best. This is not meant to imply that Knight and Smith cheat: They do not need to. It merely explains why some coaches are compelled to "lend" a young recruit $100 for a senior prom tuxedo, purchase spring break airline tickets, or provide players with occasional $500 payments (all University of Houston football program violations).[36] It explains why others may pay for rental cars, provide chauffeured limousine service, and offer $1,000 signing bonuses (as the Oklahoma University football program did).[37]

These violations may not be universal, but they do exist. It is the volume of their occurrence that provides the definitive measure of exploitation.

One hundred dollars, $500, $1,000—these figures represent tidy sums to young men from impoverished backgrounds. In mainstream American life, however, these monetary amounts are virtually meaningless. To entice a youngster by means of a car, envelopes stuffed with hundred dollar bills, or even a mysterious suitcase packed with $20,000 is nothing short of fraud. Twenty grand will get a kid a nice car, a year of partying, and maybe a few steamy romances, but it hardly prepares him for a future life. In fact, the financial and "don't-worry-about-school" inducements are tantamount to vaulting student-athletes into a state of unpreparedness, in which they expect rewards to come easily and accolades to come often. A few lucky ones, those who hit it big in pro ball, will see their expectations come to fruition. Most, however, will have to cope with life's more mundane realities: job, budget, sanity. It is here that the term exploitation is so appropriate. Athletic programs, whose survival depends on the actions of a few gifted athletes, often help to create illusions and priorities that are detrimental to the healthy, productive life of the individual participant.

CHAPTER 5

Society:
Where It All Begins

You know that ol' boy a jumpin' and a runnin' and a dunkin' . . . they say he's as dumb as a post, but he sure is a good kid.

Anonymous

This statement was overheard during a typical Southwest Missouri State University basketball practice. As is their habit on many a bleak November afternoon, the local gentlemen stroll into the university's Hammons Student Center to shoot the breeze, watch a little ball, and assess the prospects of the upcoming season's team. These men enjoy college basketball and know the game; it is the highlight of their Ozarks winter season. Particularly enjoyable to the locals is the dialogue between the coach, Charlie Spoonhour, and his players. Like many college coaches, Spoonhour has as fine a sense of humor as he does a temper. He combines the two brilliantly, much to the delight of his partisan onlookers. "Son, I believe you have broke your brain," cries the coach. Out of context, this statement hardly seems hilarious. But the sight of the short, white-haired Spoonhour ranting and raving and chasing an extremely

91

tall black kid up and down the basketball floor is more than the men of leisure can stand. They bend over, snicker, slap their thighs, exchange glances, and circle index fingers around their ears. To them, the spectacle is pure enjoyment: a bewildered and frustrated youngster, trying his hardest, and a coach, well aware of his player's effort but knowing from experience that his timely outbursts may prevent mistakes that could cost his team a ball game. It is humor based on an old theme, of which the amused may be completely unaware.

The "good kid" theory has become a staple of college athletics. The onlooker's statement, "He's as dumb as a post, but he sure is a good kid," is meant as a compliment but may actually represent the reluctant acceptance of blacks into the American mainstream. In other words, blacks are recognized as outstanding collegiate athletic participants and law-abiding citizens, but their academic involvement is viewed suspiciously, even to the point where broadcast announcers report the actual graduation of a black athlete in much the same manner as they would deliver news of a volcanic eruption on Rhode Island.

This prevailing attitude cannot be attributed to the games' participants nor to the sponsoring institutions. It is a reflection of American society in general, a society that held blacks in bondage for nearly 2 centuries and has spent another century trying to accept the fact that the former slave is the present-day equal. But the lowered expectations of latent racism are not the only negative societal influence on collegiate sports. A variety of cultural ills affect the college game and its purported academic mission, and the college game is essentially a microcosm of the culture that spawns it.

Sports are an integral facet of the American scene. They are the sole recreation for a far-too-sedentary segment of the population, and their electric atmosphere provides a suitable outlet for a stressed-out, tension-filled mass of humanity. In addition, athletics sparks both civic and national pride. A tiny Indiana community tackling urban giants in the state high school tournament and becoming the lore of book and cinema, and the 1980 United States ice hockey squad shocking the planet with its Olympic victory and eliciting a spontaneous outpouring of national button-popping and admiration, are examples of what is good and true about sports. A former "colored league" player, Ernie Banks, won the hearts of a metropolis with his boyish enthusiasm in spite of his veritable exile to the Cubs, then a bumbling, inept sports franchise. Who would have thought, a mere 20 years earlier, that a young black man from Alabama would impact Chicagoland sandlot baseball to the point where every outing was a doubleheader and every white, suburban, peewee slugger would stand in at the plate with hands back, bat perpendicular to the ground, and fingers slowly drumming the bat handle in the best Banks manner? Here is the beauty in sport. Here is its charm, its grace, its innocence. Here is the sport that promotes equality, not the sport that denies it.

Unfortunately, there is an ugly side to modern-day sports. Athletics has always been business to a certain extent, but today's athletic endeavors have definitely become big business. The profit motive has increased the necessity and importance of winning, and the "winning is everything" attitude has opened the door to the moral decay afflicting college athletics. When wins and losses are the sole gauge of accountability, athletics takes on an added seriousness. This newfound significance of sports and their heightened popularity and marketability have diminished the time-worn spirit of competition. Mere participation is no longer enough. Victory is imperative and loss is unacceptable—at least that seems to be the message that today's athletic bureaucracy is sending out.

Not only has winning become the single goal of athletics, but also, it is now accompanied by a curious lack of ethics. The two seem intertwined. As winning has been elevated to a more urgent and singular priority, the unethical attainment of this goal has become more readily acceptable. The victorious ends justify the cheating, conniving, and immoral means. Everyone should share the blame, as it is society's highly combustible mixture of a "winning is everything" attitude, unethical conduct, apathetic response, and a dose of latent racism that has hustled Division I athletics into the fast lane of distrust and paranoia.

Winning Is Everything

Winning has become the American obsession, as much a part of the national mind-set as *American Gothic* or apple pie. Our capitalist economy thrives in a defeat-and-victory environment. Our scientific and technological advancements are usually motivated by competition, be it in lunar dashes or industrial wars. Our democratic government itself consists solely of victors, and there are quite a few loyal and patriotic Americans who will forever insist that we *won* the war in Vietnam. We *are* a nation of winners and losers, and a huge amount of time and resources is spent glorifying those who come out on top. The spoils are to the victors, and the United States of America revels in the realization of this adage.

Intercollegiate athletics naturally follows course. Competition winners are placed on pedestals and treated like conquering monarchs. Trips to the White House, music-laden tributes on network TV, page after page of exploit-describing publicity in national magazines, and fat paychecks from the NCAA or bowl game sponsors are just some of the benefits reaped by winners. Transgressions are ignored, shortcomings glossed over, eyes turned the other way. Winning certainly is the American "cure for what ails ya." Of course, just make sure that you, your teammates, and your school's other programs make the winning habitual.

This deification of winning squads and their members is in itself relatively harmless. Sure, egos may be temporarily inflated, and some weighty thinkers may justifiably question the priorities involved. But adulation and praise are hardly threatening, and they do represent something positive in a world climate that is too often negative. Unfortunately, worship and celebration are not the only outcomes of the nation's addiction to winning. It is what is missing that is distressing. Those racing down the path to victory have apparently discarded some important lessons of life and have simply chosen to ignore others.

Student-athletes grow up in surroundings where losing coaches are fired, losing players are booed, and seventh-graders lacking the necessary talent are cruelly banished from organized scholastic athletics altogether. It is a tough do-or-die world, and the successful athletic competitor learns to cope and excel in it. Of course, staunch defenders of modern athletics claim that the competitive nature of sports mirrors the realities of today's world, thereby providing valuable lessons to young participants. These proponents are correct to a certain degree: There are many examples of hard-nosed competitors who have left athletics only to succeed in the political and business realms (e.g., Senator Bill Bradley and Dallas Cowboys owner Jerry Jones). However, it would seem that success in the caucus, board room, or research laboratory is of greater significance than success on the gridiron, and it would appear that many Americans have yet to make this discovery.

Americans must be world leaders in experiencing life vicariously. Whether via the curiously popular soap operas, the adventures and dangers of flashy television detectives, or the sight of young heroes doing battle for old State U, people seem most interested in the exploits of others. This helps substantiate my theory that the people of the United States are essentially a bored citizenry, which as much as anything else explains the country's increased interest in gambling, its obsession with drugs and alcohol, and its seemingly unwavering passion for television viewing.* This spectating-over-participating preference extends to the college campuses, where intramural programs are often poorly funded afterthoughts. The same school that may draw 60,000 people for a football game or 8,000 for a basketball contest may stick an intramural director in the basement of the student union, where he is understaffed and underfunded. But who can blame the institutions when they see such crass examples of commercialism as the 1987 Fiesta Bowl, where Sunkist Growers doled out $5 million to secure that year's two top football titans (Pennsylvania State University and the University of Miami) for a nation-

---

*America truly is as much The Land of the TV as it is The Land of the Free. One native television manufacturer even went so far in an endorsement as to proclaim that Americans watch more television than any other beings on the planet, as if this were something of which to be proud.

ally televised game that drew an amazing 22 million viewers, a record audience for a college football game?[1] These stratospheric dollar amounts and television audiences are not lost on revenue-seeking college administrators. This explains why big-time athletic directors have office suites rivaling those of successful corporate executives and why many intramural directors make do with converted basement storage rooms next to custodial services.

The reality behind major college athletics may be "big revenue, big television contracts, and big prestige," but to the average college fan, it is the spectacle and drama that endure.[2] Highly successful programs that, year after year, provide spectacle and drama amass legions of followers. Of course, winning is the prerequisite. The famous Ohio State University marching band script routine would hardly have the same effect if the Buckeyes did not experience such great success on the field. If the University of Arkansas's sports programs did not maintain their lofty status, wearing a plastic hog's head and screaming "pig sooey" would be laughable at best. Top Dawg would only be an obnoxiously goofy mascot if Billy Tubbs's Oklahoma University Sooners did not rampage up and down the basketball court with such élan. But these programs remain successful, and their symbols and traditions inspire reverence more often than mockery. These "rich, winning traditions," as they are so often called, inspire other things, too—notably, a single-minded lust for winning.

Winning at Oklahoma

Nowhere is the serious let's-kick-some-ass attitude more apparent than in Oklahoma, where the Oklahoma University football Sooners have run roughshod over less endowed opponents for nearly 2 decades. Sooner football is a passion within Oklahoma's boundaries, and it is what the state is best known for, along with oil rigs and dust storms. Six national championships in the last 3 decades, numerous Big Eight Conference championships, and many a game where the Sooners' vaunted wishbone offense has crushed outmanned opponents in the 60–0 range—all these things have added to the OU football lore. The Okies love it, too (with the exception of a rebellious little pocket around Stillwater, home of Oklahoma State): The bigger the margin of victory the better, and, in the mind of the citizenry, the less tarnished is the state by the *Grapes of Wrath* inferiority complex that has agitated the Oklahoma psyche for many years. It does not matter that Colorado University students once held up a banner proclaiming, "WE WOULD RATHER LOSE TO OKLAHOMA THAN LIVE THERE." Sooner fans recognized that as a mere expression of jealousy.

Still, one would think that the off-the-field exploits of the Sooner program and its players would be enough to somewhat cool the fans' lust for

"How Much Is That Doggie in the Window?"

Texas A&M University has one of those "rich, winning, traditions" and a colorful history of school spirit. Students stand throughout the game, male yell leaders perform in traditional fashion, dates kiss after touchdowns, and the Aggie band draws standing ovations in opponents' stadiums. So it should come as no surprise to learn that the school mascot is the recipient of much adulation.

Several years ago, the beloved Texas A&M mascot, Reveille, died of natural causes. According to Texas football lore, devotion and respect for the animal were so great that his death was literally mourned by thousands, who viewed the deceased canine as he lay in state. The following weekend found the Aggies traveling south to Houston to battle the Rice football Owls. Texas A&M was administering its annual butt kicking when the onslaught was mercifully interrupted by the halftime festivities. As is the tradition, the visiting team's band put on the first halftime performance. High-stepping with energetic precision, the Aggie band performed like clockwork. Normally this would be a tough act for the somewhat disorganized and often irreverent Rice band to follow, but the Owl musicians were not to be upstaged on this day. After the Aggie martial performance, the Rice band members sauntered onto the field while the announcer proclaimed that the band would salute the late Reveille with a musical tribute. The sentimental A&M faithful, nearly half of those in attendance, stood solemnly with moist eyes. Then, on cue, the Rice band raced into formation—a giant fire hydrant—and proceeded to play "How Much is That Doggie in the Window?" The Aggie fans were so shocked and outraged by this performance, which they considered blasphemous, that the second half of the game became irrelevant, a nuisance as they tried to express their anger. By game's end, the Texas A&M Cadets and alumni had driven themselves into a bloodthirsty frenzy. The Rice band was forced to leave their own stadium under police escort to ensure the members' safety.

Maybe the Rice band's performance was a little tasteless, but the mere fact that a musical joke could incite a near riot says something important about today's athletics. The levity is gone, the sportsmanship is lacking, and winning—as long as the right team does it—is all that matters.

the game, or at least cause some quiet consideration over the program's ethics. It would seem that 6 years on NCAA probation since 1976, a multitude of criminal offenses by Sooner players ranging from drugs to violence to rape, and an administration's and coaching staff's win-at-all-costs attitude would weaken the public's confidence and cause negative backlash.[3] But that simply has not been the case.

Until Coach Barry Switzer's 1989 resignation from frustration and burnout, the only time he and his staff were *seriously* in jeopardy was after the 1983 season, when the Sooners posted an extremely disappointing 8-4 record. Even the 1988–89 Sooner crime spree involving alleged shooting, drug sale, and gang rape never actually threatened to topple the "Football Is King" empire, as long as Switzer promised to clean up his act a little. Certainly, Switzer and his program came under widespread media criticism, but few Oklahomans were ready to admit that they and their national championship tunnel vision were the real culprits in the Sooner tragedy. This, of course, is symptomatic of what *Sports Illustrated* so aptly described as the "Oklahoma malady: blind love for the Sooners."[4]

Oklahoma Is Not OK

The 1988–89 season will never be remembered as a vintage year for the University of Oklahoma football program. The NCAA placed the Sooner football program on 3 years' probation for "major violations," but that was merely the harbinger of things to come. On January 13, redshirt freshman cornerback Jerry Parks shot teammate Zarak Peters in the chest after an argument in their dormitory. Eight days later three players, Glen Bell, Nigel Clay, and Bernard Hall, were arraigned on charges of rape. As if these sordid affairs were not enough, the very next week found starting quarterback Charles Thompson under arrest for selling 17 grams of cocaine to an undercover agent. Oklahoma University's then interim president David Swan responded to the episodes by telling *Sports Illustrated* reporter Rick Telander that they were merely "isolated incidents."

Winning at Kentucky

Oklahoma University is not the only institution afflicted with such a myopic viewpoint. Numerous other Division I behemoths are susceptible to the same problem; the University of Kentucky Wildcats are another unsavory example.

Basketball and horses are the primary fare in the Bluegrass State, and longtime Kentucky coach Adolph Rupp was largely responsible for at least half of this situation. Rupp was the roundball king (some would say dictator) of the South, and his Wildcats had many seasons where they led wire to wire, developing a fervent statewide and regional following. Some of Rupp's practices were rumored to be less than scrupulous, but he was a state icon and was regarded as virtually untouchable.

After Rupp's retirement, Joe B. Hall took over the Kentucky program. Hall carried on the Kentucky tradition by guiding his team to the 1978 NCAA National Championship, and plans were in the making to construct a cavernous 21,000-seat arena honoring the late Rupp. However, Hall's stranglehold was not as tight as Rupp's, and critics began to chip away at the Kentucky program. The criticism culminated in a 1986 media exposure of various NCAA infractions committed by the university's basketball program. Although the *Lexington Herald-Leader* won a Pulitzer Prize for its investigative reporting, the story was met with harsh criticism from the Wildcat faithful, who went so far as to issue death threats against the journalists involved. Naturally, the brouhaha led to an NCAA investigation, but a massive cover-up ensued in which original sources forgot prior testimony or denied previous statements. It was not until nearly 3 years later that, amidst a plethora of allegations, the notorious Kentucky program toppled under the relatively less successful reign of coach Eddie Sutton.

The Costs of the Winning-Is-Everything Philosophy

What are the ramifications of the win-at-all-costs and winning-is-everything attitudes? At the very least, they undermine the academic purpose of the institution, and at their worst, they taint a golden opportunity for disadvantaged youngsters. Perhaps Jerry Kirshenbaum portrayed the situation most accurately when he wrote:

> Let's look at what intercollegiate athletics is about. College presidents and athletic directors will tell you that their sports programs develop school spirit, raise money for other purposes and enhance their institution's image. What they mean is that winning does all that. And because not everyone can win, the scramble to do so leads many schools to commit deeds that have exactly the opposite effect.[5]

These "deeds that have exactly the opposite effect" mirror a serious lack of ethics in American society. Consider the case of Colonel Oliver North, who in his ballyhooed 1989 trial admitted to lying to Congress and blatantly disregarding other accepted codes of behavior. Maintaining that his actions were justified by the pressing national security issues of the time, North was defended by many as a great American patriot.

Consider the fact that, despite the widening gap between the well-off and the disenfranchised poor and the loss of financial ground by our public schools due to inflation and sinking state revenues, state after state has passed tax reform laws making it increasingly difficult to systematically raise much-needed money for the schools or the poor. Although the official rationale for the tax revolution speaks of wasteful spending and conjures images of the Boston Tea Party, the actual motivation is simple and unadulterated greed.

Consider the case of the University of Georgia when, in its defense during the infamous 1986 Jan Kemp trial, it claimed it *had* to act disreputably in the recruitment and retention of student-athletes to compete with rivals who were doing the same. Consider Barry Switzer's response when asked why he recruited a player with a history of unstable behavior who eventually shot and seriously wounded a teammate: "Everyone else wanted him. He was highly recruited. He would've played for another school."[6] These are the lessons in ethics that society provides for its youth; these are the "ethical" practices of the sometimes less-than-admirable NCAA membership.

Moral Delinquency

The notion that the United States is becoming an ethical wasteland is neither new nor surprising, but the expectation that intercollegiate athletics and its participants should rise from the muck that envelops the rest of society is extremely hypocritical. Why should a nation that spawns million-dollar Give-Me-That-Old-Time-Religion crooks expect superior behavior from an athletic director? Why should a nation that elects presidents who lie outright or feign loss of memory expect forthrightness from a Division I basketball coach? And why should a nation whose habits fuel illegal billion-dollar industries in drugs, gambling, and prostitution expect abstinence from 19-year-olds? As *Sports Illustrated* writers Rick Telander and Robert Sullivan observed about the Oklahoma University football program, "You reap what you sow." What our society has reaped is a blighted athletic crop of some administrators, coaches, athletes, and boosters to whom ethics mean little.

Although the idea that participants in NCAA Division I men's athletics have ethical shortcomings may seem distasteful to some and preposterous to others, evidence suggests that this may be the case. A 1987 Texas Tech University study found that male Division I athletes displayed lower levels of moral reasoning than did female Division I athletes or their "noncompetitive peers." The study, conducted by associate professor and sports sociologist Elizabeth R. Hall, asked 64 Division I basketball players a series of sports and nonsports questions intended to shed light on a player's level of moral reasoning. The questions were designed to focus more on *why* something might be right or wrong than on what is right or wrong in itself. For example, "a person who says stealing is wrong because you might get caught scores lower than a person who says stealing is wrong because it hurts society."[7]

The researcher believed that differences in the "male and female athletic environments" might explain the men's lower moral reasoning levels. In Hall's view, less intense pressure to win—on female coaches and players alike—resulted in a less "oppressive" atmosphere. Her findings also suggested that "authoritarian leadership, competitiveness, and sports' winning-is-everything ethic contribute to the lower reasoning ability of athletes."[8]

The findings of one isolated study hardly constitute irrefutable evidence that male student-athletes are lacking in morality or ethics, but people denying the existence of an ethical void in college athletics might as well bury their heads with the rest of the ostriches. Consider the following occurrence and its underlying message. Norm Stewart's 1984–85 Missouri Tigers were relegated to the National Invitational Tourney (NIT), where they hosted Philadelphia's St. Joseph College Hawks in a first-round game at MU's Hearnes Center. Missouri's players approached the contest with all the vigor and enthusiasm of a teenager taking out the trash, and the underdog Hawks quickly built a substantial first-half lead. The St. Joseph squad maintained the margin into the second half before they were met by a furious rally from a suddenly inspired Missouri team. The younger Hawks became flustered and disorganized as the veteran Tigers applied intense and disciplined defensive pressure. Still, the double-digit gap represented a long haul for Missouri, and there were only 4 seconds left on the clock when the Tigers took a 1-point lead for the first time in the game.

St. Joseph would have one last desperation shot. They passed the ball near the midcourt line, where a player took a couple of dribbles and heaved the ball toward the goal. The ball clanged up and off the rim, the buzzer sounded, and another St. Joseph player belatedly tipped the ball into the basket as if out of frustration. But wait: The officials remained on the floor, and there was no referee signal that the game had officially ended. All eyes in the arena eventually focused on a chubby little official standing in the middle of the court. After a couple of seconds that seemed like an eternity, the befuddled referee put his right hand high in the air, jerked down violently, and dashed off the floor, wisely seeking refuge.

Pandemonium ensued. The Missouri coaches took off at a sprint, presumably to strangle the quickly waddling official. Veins bulged in the necks of irate Missouri boosters. St. Joseph's players and coaches mimicked the Watusi as they celebrated at midcourt. The scene took on a farcical nature, which was only appropriate because the official had atrociously blown the call. It was beyond doubt that the buzzer had sounded before the ball was tipped, at least a full second before. How or why the official made the call is pure conjecture. What is certain, though, is the event's underlying significance. Here were the St. Joseph coaches and players, knowing full well that they had actually *lost* the game, but celebrating as if they had earned a national championship. It did not seem to matter to them that the game had ended unfairly, that in reality they had been defeated. It only seemed to matter that, in the record books, the big *W* would be recorded.

Where was the sportsmanship? Where was the fairness? Where was the honesty? Undoubtedly, the St. Joseph coaches would claim that justice had prevailed, and they would point to several questionable calls during Missouri's frantic comeback. But such rationalization is hardly the point. The point is that modern intercollegiate athletics is so obsessed with winning that winning fairly or acting ethically is hardly a consideration. Instead of going to the scorer's table and admitting they had actually lost the game, St. Joseph's coaches dashed off the court, taking a *W* any way they could get it. This signal, being sent to many players, is a primary reason why some student-athletes display questionable conduct in academic and social spheres.

While the symptoms receive sensational, albeit temporary media highlighting, the disease itself goes virtually unnoticed. Most literate people are certainly aware of the abuses and scandals in intercollegiate athletics, but they seem ignorant of the various factors that spawn them. If people are aware of the societal mind-set and cultural influences that dictate the unethical pursuit of intercollegiate athletic victory, they are completely apathetic about them.

Of course, the presence of apathy should not come as a great surprise. Next to the growth of state lotteries, apathy may well be the nation's fastest-surging trend. Whether the event is a cataclysmic oil spill, the depletion of ozone layers or rain forests, or lying and cheating by federal administrators, the obvious fact is that very few people seem to care. This don't-give-a-damn attitude has unquestionably and naturally infiltrated college athletics. Oh, sure, the glossy news coverage of misdeeds evokes words of reform and fiery outrage, but the furor is short-lived. Few people care to examine the problems long enough or closely enough to develop insightful understanding or meaningful solutions.

Racism in Athletics

A smart college basketball coach plays three blacks at home, four on the road, and five when he is behind.

A long-standing joke often attributed
to former collegiate and NBA great
Bill Russell.

Thriving in the atmosphere of apathy and corruption is the latent racism that permeates American sports, intercollegiate athletics in particular. Today's racism for the most part is not as overt, restrictive, or physically discriminatory as it was in past decades. It is more passive, less conscious and tangible. Still, it is every bit as harmful.

Play-by-play commentator: You know, Marv, that Johnson kid has catlike quickness.

Color commentator: His hands are the size of ice tongs, Bob. Kind of reminds me of the days when they would deliver blocks of ice to my grandmother's house.

Play-by-play commentator: He's really handling the ball now. He just has excellent instincts for the game.

Color commentator: They say he's going to graduate, too.

This type of nonsensical dialogue can be heard hundreds of times during the winter college basketball season. Night after night, over cable, the networks, and local media outlets, one nondescript announcer after another describes game after game, making the same observations and using the same clichés. The preceding dialogue may be fictitious, but it might well be heard as Seton Hall plays Georgetown, Ball State meets Miami of Ohio, or Southern Utah State takes on Northern Arizona. You can also bet that the described player is black, as the language, the metaphors, and the analogies always give his race away. "Catlike quickness" and hands "the size of ice tongs" typify the animal and machine images often used to describe the black player. The player also has "excellent instincts," not intelligence; the intelligence label is usually reserved for the black athlete's white teammate. Of course, the word *instincts* is sometimes omitted, and on these occasions, a black player's headiness may be attributed to "breeding" or to "genes" from a father who was a former successful athlete. Finally, there is the clause, "he's going to graduate, too," as though it were a given that all black athletes would not. Some might deem these examples trivial or mere slips of the tongue, but they are much more. Language has the power to shape concepts, and the constant comparison of blacks to animals or inert objects, however unconscious or unintentional, dehumanizes the black athlete and creates a public stereotype of the black young man as having few gifts besides athletic prowess.

Texas Western's 1966 NCAA National Championship in basketball marked a watershed year for blacks in intercollegiate athletics. In an event described as the "*Brown v. Board of Education* of college basketball,"[9] Texas Western's five black starters defeated the five white starters of Adolph Rupp's seemingly invincible University of Kentucky team. Although the surly Rupp attempted to discredit Texas Western's victory by claiming that they used players "out of the Tennessee penitentiary and off the streets of New York,"[10] the title remained the property of the lesser known Texas institution. Texas Western's successful reliance on black athletes opened the doors for traditional white intercollegiate programs to recruit more and more black players. Of course, the Rupp attitude remained quite prevalent. While the past 2 decades have softened it somewhat, their passing has not completely eliminated it.

Rupp's scorn of the black athlete is still secretly harbored by many Americans. While they are less vocal and fewer in numbers, their presence, combined with that of many people who possess a subconscious or latent racist attitude, forms quite a barrier to the unanimous and equitable acceptance of black participation in sports. The historical roots of this attitude go deep. Consider the views of Carl Campbell Brigham, author of the 1923 book *A Study of American Intelligence*. David Owen describes the writer and his text:

> Brigham reserved most of his considerable scorn for blacks, whose arrival in America he described as, "the most sinister development in the history of the continent." In charts and graphs and throughout his text, he repeatedly treated blacks (and Jews) as being distinct from "Americans." Indeed, he seems to have considered blacks to be members of a separate species, referring at one point to the "sub-species" of various races. He quoted very approvingly a passage from a recent book by Edwin G. Conklin, a colleague at Princeton, in which Conklin advocated "geographical isolation of the races" in order to "prevent their inbreeding" but despaired that it might be only temporarily possible to maintain "purity of the white race."[11]

Brigham furthered his position by writing that the "dilution of the master race" was directly related to abolition during the Civil War—all this from a man whom the College Board hired to develop the SAT.[12] As Paul Harvey might say, "And now you know the rest of the story."

That a prominent, respected psychologist advocated such insidiously racist views a mere 60 years (only three generations) ago dramatizes the magnitude of the hurdles that have faced the black population and ultimately the nation as a whole. Brigham might find himself ostracized for espousing such views today, but the residual racist attitude still exists. These feelings "buttress notions of race-linked black proclivities for both athletic prowess and intellectual deficiency."[13]

These notions, sadly, provide the black student-athlete with a way out, a cop-out, a convenient excuse for avoiding effort and success in the academic arena. One black Southwest Missouri State student-athlete blamed a poor grade on the fact that his professor was a "George Wallace dude who won't give the brothers a break." True or not, a break was not what this particular student needed. What he did need was a kick in the pants. And if his instructor truly did act in a racially biased manner, a strong classroom effort and a solid academic performance would have been the best way to prove the instructor wrong.

The common American image of the good ol' boy suggests lazy small-town streets, a *Reader's Digest* on the coffee table, a baseball game on the radio, and a pool game and a beer—both on tap later in the evening at a nearby bar and grill. A more upscale version of the scene would include a small-town country club with a gin game and a par five that plays tough when the creek is up, a Winnebago with a portable TV, and a fall trip over to Knoxville to watch the Tennessee Volunteers lock face masks with the Crimson Tide: yes, siree—Bob, 90,000 good ol' boys intently watching the not-so-childlike antics of 50 or so "good kids." But being a good kid is not enough anymore. Being allowed in the school or on the court is not enough anymore, either. Even "actin' decent and respectable" just won't cut the mustard. Black student-athletes, all student-athletes, must rise above the mediocre expectations people have for them—especially because mediocre expectations bring mediocre results. They must not allow the lingering doubts of others to become modern-day shackles.

CHAPTER 6

Solving the Problems, or Creating New Ones?

Although a true understanding of the academic dilemma facing college athletics is rare, there is undeniably a widespread awareness that a serious problem exists. It would be almost impossible to believe otherwise. Drug abuse, scheming agents, unjustified violence, and academic improprieties have all been reported by the media. An average American may not be cognizant of the individual, institutional, and societal factors underlying these problems, but they do know that the Boz took steroids and that Len Bias died of a cocaine overdose during a period when he was failing to attend his University of Maryland classes. This is particularly bad publicity for the NCAA and America's institutions of higher education. Their motives have been criticized as unprincipled; their integrity has been questioned.

The NCAA and the institutions *have* responded, although the degree and rapidity of these responses have also been subject to disapproval. Studies, meetings, rules, and legislation have all been part of a somewhat-less-than-coordinated effort to thwart the apparent evils that are threatening college athletic programs and the schools that support them. More than anything else, there has been rhetoric. But there is some tangible evidence that a movement is afoot to rectify the problems

---

The Boz

Brian Bosworth was an outspoken and extremely talented linebacker at the University of Oklahoma. He sported a techno-robotic look, and his taunting of opponents was as outrageous as his hairstyle. In reality, Bosworth was a good student who was milking the media for all it was worth, and some people tolerated his behavior much as one puts up with a spoiled brat. The Boz's act took a dive, though, when before the 1987 Orange Bowl he tested positive for steroid use. Relegated to the sideline during the game, Bosworth wore a profane T-shirt expressing his feelings toward the NCAA. This prompted Switzer, in a rare act of discipline, to kick his All-American linebacker off the team. Bosworth then went to the Seattle Seahawks of the NFL, where his highly publicized career was one of the biggest professional busts of the '80s.

---

related to the erosion of academics in the athletic realm. Groups, forums, and commissions (including the influential Presidents Commission) have been assembled and called to order. NCAA legislation mandating stricter rules and regulations has been proposed, debated, and sometimes passed. Even the federal government is considering involvement, as various legislators discuss some curious forms of arguably intrusive legislation. And the universities themselves—culprits or victims, depending on one's perspective—are trying to remedy the situation with various academic advisement and support programs.

None of these actions has been overwhelmingly successful in silencing intercollegiate athletics' harshest critics, but the efforts do represent the sincere concern of many responsible individuals. Still, as in many other reforms and attempts to cure specific social ills, the mood is too hurried, the goals too shortsighted, and a far too superficial grasp of the problem leaves the involved parties with the reform equivalent of placing Band-Aids on a battleship.

Educational Reform by Committee

Throughout American bureaucratic history, social maladies have triggered the formation of fact-finding committees. Their membership rosters have been dotted with the names of esteemed citizens, and they have often met under pretentious circumstances, issuing voluminous and sometimes pompous reports. Their various recommendations have sometimes been implemented, but more often than not they have served only to inspire more rhetoric. And the result? Life goes on pretty much as it always has.

National Commission on Excellence in Education

The widely publicized 1983 report, *A Nation at Risk*, is an excellent example of this scenario. The National Commission on Excellence in Education was appointed by the Reagan administration to examine the state of American education. Composed of influential educational and business leaders, the commission met several times and eventually issued the much-anticipated *A Nation at Risk* report, a document intended to change the face of the nation's schooling. Damning, critical, foreboding—but primarily presumptuous—the report compared the state of the public schools to the aftermath of a foreign invasion and predicted dire consequences for the United States and practically the entire free world. Much media attention was focused on the study, and it was not long before everyone from Paul Harvey to Nancy Reagan became an educational expert jumping on the nation-at-risk bandwagon.

The report did have its repercussions. Education became more politicized, tougher academic standards were adopted, and educators were supposedly held more accountable—whatever that means. Still, the nature of American schooling changed little if at all. In most elementary classrooms, groups of about 30 kids continued to sit in rows and listen to teachers talk during the majority of the school day. Most high schools were still populated by a few kids who truly wanted to be there, a few kids who certainly did not, and a whole bunch in the middle who were not sure what was going on. And most colleges and universities still scampered along the treadmill of trying to be all things to all people. Realistically, in spite of *A Nation at Risk*'s vitriolic language and general distribution, *true* reform has been nonexistent or is at least slow in coming.

Ad Hoc Committee on the Problems of Major Intercollegiate Athletic Programs

The leaders of the NCAA and of America's universities and colleges can never be accused of being ahistorical; their knowledge of the past must be great, to judge by the course of their actions. As the publicity surrounding intercollegiate athletics' shortcomings mounted to the point of creating a public furor, these leaders stayed the traditional course by forming committees to look into problems and propose solutions. One of the first and, in retrospect, most influential groups was the American Council on Education (ACE) and its Ad Hoc Committee on the Problems of Major Intercollegiate Athletic Programs. Founded in 1918, the American Council on Education represents nearly 1,600 colleges and universities. Its purported philosophy is "to advance education . . . through comprehensive, voluntary, and cooperative action on the part of American educational associations, organizations, and institutions . . . [and to] serve education in such undertakings as may be required and approved from year to year and from generation to generation for the common welfare."[1] These are lofty goals, and apparently the ACE felt that an examination of intercollegiate athletics was well within its mission.

The Ad Hoc Committee was formed in 1982 to give campus executives a new forum to deal with college athletics, which had been tainted by charges of recruitment violation, illegal payment to student-athletes, tampering with academic records, and other irregularities. Harvard University president Derek Bok chaired the committee, which initially comprised 40 college and university presidents. By September of 1982, committee members had written proposals that would toughen eligibility and academic progress rules for student-athletes. It was decided that the committee would introduce two proposals to the 1983 NCAA January convention. They were as follows:

> 1. An initial eligibility standard for Division I intercollegiate athletics, commencing in 1986, would combine a minimum grade point average in a core curriculum of high school courses with minimum standardized test scores.
>
> 2. To remain eligible for varsity competition after the freshman year, a student-athlete would—in addition to meeting all existing NCAA requirements—have to make satisfactory progress toward a baccalaureate degree and be in good academic standing as certified by appropriate academic authorities.[2]

The Ad Hoc Committee later elaborated on these proposals by seeking NCAA legislation requiring a prospective student-athlete to graduate from high school with at least a 2.0 grade point average on a 4.0 scale in a core curriculum of 11 academic courses. This core curriculum was to consist at minimum of three English courses, two mathematics courses, two social science courses, and two courses in the natural or physical sciences. In addition, a combined score of 700 would be required on the Scholastic Aptitude Test (SAT) or a composite score of 15 on the American College Testing Program (ACT) exam. These Ad Hoc Committee proposals would eventually become the foundation for future reform and would be realized in the form of the much-discussed and controversial Proposition 48.

The committee's emphasis on academics was "natural," according to Harvard CEO Bok and ACE leader J. W. Petalson, former president of the University of Illinois:

> [A]s educators these are the topics where we have the greatest expertise and for which we have a clear and inescapable responsibility to assert the supremacy of academic values. We are concerned that in the zeal to produce winning teams, athletic eligibility has often been placed ahead of academic qualification.

The concern with eligibility also results in some athletes being counseled to take courses which may not satisfy a degree program.[3]

Bok's and Petalson's concern for academic integrity was undoubtedly legitimate, but author Linda Greene believes that the college presidents had an ulterior motive. Greene wrote in the *Saint Louis University Law Journal* that the committee's concern for academic issues was more than likely surpassed by its distress over a "more pressing objective: repair of damage to the credibility of universities and colleges due to repeated sports scandals."[4]

This accusation that the Ad Hoc Committee was essentially concerned with the rapid formulation of a sugar-coated panacea for a worsening public relations malaise may be an accurate criticism of the committee's deliberations. Proposition 48—the merits of which will be discussed later in more detail—was at best a quick-fix solution that focused on quantifiable student characteristics rather than deeply ingrained educational problems facing many prospective student-athletes. Still, the Ad Hoc Committee drew even more fiery scorn over another concern: lack of representation from historically black institutions and the fact that the committee failed to include a single black representative.

As hard as it may be to believe, there was, in fact, no black representation whatsoever as the Ad Hoc Committee was formulating its proposals for the 1983 NCAA convention. On such an emotionally charged issue, the exclusion of black input seems incredible and inexcusable. But ACE and NCAA representatives expressed surprise that the committee's proposals were viewed in a racial light.[5] All this admittance of surprise amounts to, though, is a confession that little forethought went into the entire proposal formulation procedure. The fact that black educational leaders such as Southern University president Jesse Stone were completely unaware of the proposals until only a couple of months before the NCAA convention points to irresponsibility and elitism.[6]

Just before the convention, the Ad Hoc Committee did finally extend an invitation to a black representative, Luna I. Mishoe, president of Delaware State University. But the groundwork for the proposals had already been laid, and Mishoe would eventually and quite openly voice his opposition to the entire proceedings. That any legislation with such ramifications for the black community could be drawn up and finally enacted with such minimal black involvement is an utter sham and a disgrace to higher education. It is reason enough for serious and critical review of the Proposition 48 legislation and the procedures behind its adoption.

The success of the ACE Ad Hoc Committee's initiatives represented the vulnerability of the NCAA to powerful outside organizations. Therefore, the NCAA, in an effort to save face and retain power, has allied itself more closely with its academic colleagues. This alliance has resulted in the current NCAA Presidents Commission, a group of institutional leaders whose duty it is to work closely with the athletic organization's membership to ensure academic integrity and explore avenues for improving intercollegiate sports in general. The commission has several committees, each of which has several task forces. An example of this structure was the 1989 move by the NCAA Presidents Commission's Advisory Committee to Review the Governance Process to form three separate task forces charged with examining the NCAA legislative process, the role of chief executive officers in the governance process, and the "nature" and "atmosphere" of NCAA conventions.[7] If this all sounds like so much bureaucratic gobbledygook, it probably is. But the increased interaction between university academic leaders and the athletic organization is a step in the right direction.

The great irony of the NCAA is that while its activities are enjoying their greatest-ever profitability and popularity, the organization has been coming under ever-increasing criticism. There is something unusual about this, and there might be a tendency for the organization to develop a Standard-Oil-as-the-big-bad-monopoly chip on the shoulder. That has not happened, however, and the NCAA should be commended for it. Instead, the "amateur" organization has funneled vast amounts of its huge earnings into research and programs to counteract some of the less-than-admirable trends seen in today's intercollegiate games.

American Institutes for Research Study

One of the most prodigious and costly endeavors of the NCAA was the year-long $1.75 million research study conducted by the American Institutes for Research (AIR) for the association.[8] "An independent, not-for-profit, behavior-science research organization,"[9] AIR obtained data from more than 4,000 student-athletes and other students to interpret the "complex picture that emerges of students who participate in major college athletics programs."[10] The study (highlighted in chapter 2) produced no radically surprising findings but did represent a more scholarly and sagacious approach to remedying current intercollegiate athletic-academic difficulties. Particularly positive was the release in the spring of 1989 of data pertaining to black student-athletes. The admittance that many black athletes are "less well-prepared for college studies" and come from "homes with lower socioeconomic status than their non-black teammates"[11] is a positive move toward getting at the root of the NCAA's problem.

The NCAA: Getting Its Own House in Order

The NCAA has devoted a great deal of its time, energy, and resources to dealing with the academic issues of intercollegiate sports. Proposal

---

Some Interesting Statistics From the American Institutes for Research Study[a]

According to the 1989 American Institutes for Research study, 12 percent of the U.S. population at that time was black. Of the people enrolled in Division I institutions, 4 percent were black. Considering those statistics, note the following:

- Of the athletes in Division I institutions . . .
  . . . 37 percent of football players were black.
  . . . 56 percent of men's basketball players were black.
  . . . 33 percent of women's basketball players were black.
- 49 percent of black football and basketball players rank in the lowest socioeconomic quartile.
- 35 percent of black athletes in other sports rank in the lowest socioeconomic quartile.
- Only 13 percent of nonblack football and basketball players are in the lowest socioeconomic quartile.
- 58 percent of black football and basketball players had SAT scores in the lowest quartile.
- 35 percent of black athletes in other sports had SAT scores in the lowest quartile.
- Only 19 percent of nonblack football and basketball players had SAT scores in the lowest quartile.
- 61 percent of black football and basketball players had a B-minus or lower GPA in high school.
- 35 percent of black athletes in other sports had a B-minus or lower GPA in high school.
- 31 percent of nonblack football and basketball players had a B-minus or lower GPA in high school.

Note. [a]"Research Institute Releases Study of Black Student-Athletes," *The NCAA News*, 5 April 1989, 19.

---

after proposal has been debated, passed, or voted down, and the association has hired a veritable army of bright, energetic enforcement bloodhounds who scour the member institutions seeking out wrongdoing and academic skullduggery. The resulting actions, though, have all too often been punitive in nature: For example, if a student-athlete does this, then this result occurs; if a member institution does this, then this sanction is leveled against it. The association has done little to expose the essence of the problem—to treat the disease instead of the symptoms. Certainly, the reams of pages that make up the *NCAA Manual* represent concern for the student-athlete on the part of the association and its members, and maybe the complex issues surrounding minority student-athletes are beyond the scope of the NCAA. But 400 pages filled with legalese descriptions of incomprehensible legislation mean little for an 18-year-old basketball player. Some serious introspection by the NCAA into what and how it has evolved might be more meaningful than all of the *NCAA Manuals* and the rules they contain.

Proposition 48 Explained

Proposition 48 is the ultimate NCAA regulation to dissect. There are a multitude of other rules and regulations pertaining to academic eligibility and athletic participation, but no other rule has been so publicized, discussed, consequential, or indicative of the NCAA's response to public pressure. Proposition 48 is the symbol of the association's reform efforts. Its examination sheds light on the attitude of the NCAA and the mistakes the organization has made in trying to legislate academic integrity. Proposition 48 (formerly Bylaw 5-1-(j), now officially known as Bylaws 14.3.1 and 14.3.2) was, as previously detailed, the product of the American Council on Education's Ad Hoc Committee on the Problems of Major Intercollegiate Athletic Programs. The committee's concern for the academic integrity of intercollegiate sports led to the proposal of legislation that would tighten entrance eligibility requirements for Division I freshman athletes. The proposal, which focused on core requirements, high school grade point averages, and the standardized test scores of prospective student-athletes, was passed at the NCAA convention held in San Diego from January 10 to 12, 1983.[12] The legislation, which emerged from a turbulent cloud of controversy, now reads as follows:

> 14.3.1 ELIGIBILITY FOR FINANCIAL AID AND COMPETITION. A student-athlete who enrolls in a Division I or Division II institution as an entering freshman with no previous full-time college attendance shall meet the following academic requirements, and any applicable institutional and conference regulations, to be considered a qualifier and thus be eligible for financial aid, practice and competition during the first academic year in residence. B5-1-(j)-(1)

> 14.3.1.1 QUALIFIER, BASIC REQUIREMENTS. A qualifier is defined as one who is a high school graduate and who presented the following academic qualifications: B5-1-(j)-Note

> (a) A minimum cumulative grade-point average of 2.000 (based on a maximum of 4.000) in a successfully completed core curriculum of at least 11 academic courses, including at least the following:

English	3 years
Mathematics	2 years
Social science	2 years
Natural or physical science (including at least one laboratory course, if offered by the high school)	2 years

The record of the above courses and course grades must be certified on the high school transcript or by official correspondence, and

(b) A minimum 700 combined score on the SAT verbal and math sections, or a minimum 18 composite score on the ACT. The required SAT or ACT score must be achieved under normal testing conditions on a national testing date [i.e., no residual (campus) testing]. B5-1-(j)-Note-(i), LA86-29

14.3.2 ELIGIBILITY FOR FINANCIAL AID, PRACTICE AND COMPETITION—PARTIAL QUALIFIER AND NONQUALIFIER

14.3.2.1 PARTIAL QUALIFIER An entering freshman with no previous college attendance who enrolls in a Division I or Division II institution and who is a partial qualifier (as defined in 14.02.9.2) may receive institutional financial aid (see 15.02.3.1) based on institutional and conference regulations but may not practice or compete during the first academic year in residence. B5-1-(j)-(2)[13]

This is Proposition 48 in all of its glory, and it offered the American sports scene a new set of labels including the terms *qualifier, partial qualifier*, and *nonqualifier*. Qualifiers meet all the requirements of Proposition 48 and are therefore eligible to compete as freshmen and receive financial aid through athletic scholarships. Partial qualifiers are potential student-athletes who do not meet all of the requirements of Proposition 48 (Bylaw 14.3.1) but have earned an overall grade point average of 2.000 or better in high school. These so-called partial qualifiers may only receive need-based, nonathletically-related financial aid, but not athletically-related aid. They are ineligible to compete as freshmen and, contingently upon their passing 24 credit hours in their first year, are allowed only 3 years of eligibility thereafter. Finally, a nonqualifier is simply ineligible for any type of athletic scholarship and must go the junior college or NAIA route.

Oddly enough, NCAA Division II schools were originally excluded from the 1983 Proposition 48 standards. However, in January 1987, after lengthy debate followed by a close vote, the Division II schools agreed to adhere to the Proposition 48 standards.[14] Even the more loosely knit and less bureaucratic NAIA eventually set minimum academic guidelines, although they appeared to be somewhat oblique. Obviously, everyone was following the Division I lead, and they could ill afford not to because of the public outcry over academic abuses in college sports. But the urge to jump on the bandwagon and to maintain public relations integrity was not the sole motivating force behind the adoption of the stricter rules. Proposition 48 supporters seemed to believe unanimously that "reasonable academic success should be prerequisite for students wishing to participate" in intercollegiate sports.[15]

There seemed to be plenty of evidence in support of this position, too. Take the case of former University of Arkansas basketball player Dean Tolson. Tolson, a 6'8" center who had a vagabond-like professional career, left the Fayetteville campus in 1974 with a 1.43 GPA that included 38 credit hours of F. How the University of Arkansas maintained Tolson's eligibility seems a question of little significance as one examines Tolson's high school transcript. The transcript, dotted with courses like metal shop, auto mechanics, printing, cooking, speech, and family relations, is hardly representative (except for speech) of a high school career that could adequately prepare a student for the rigors of college.[16] The fact that Tolson's overall high school grade point average was 1.83 is also suspicious. Such course work and lackadaisical performance were the very things that the Proposition 48 proponents were hoping to eliminate. As Arkansas athletic director and former Razorback football coach Frank Broyles readily and candidly admitted in *Sports Illustrated*, "In the '70s, all of us in athletics found ways to take advantage of school rules to keep athletes eligible. A coach did all he could to save his job. We just jumped at great athletes. Dean was enrolled in classes only to stay eligible; he made no progress toward a degree. That was within NCAA rules."[17] These lax NCAA rules were the very targets of the Ad Hoc Committee and its supporters.

Despite the apparent logic of the new academic standards and the fine intentions of their supporters, both continued to come under blistering attack. The most vociferous detractors were blacks and the historically black colleges and universities. They believed, and justifiably so, that Proposition 48 could be the death knell for their already struggling and financially shaky athletic programs. Once proud and talent-rich, the Gramblings, Prairie View A&Ms, and North Carolina A&Ts had seen their competitive caliber severely eroded by the mass exodus of the South's most talented black athletes to the wealthier, more prestigious white schools, which had previously featured Caucasian athletes. Now, under the new Prop 48 standards, many of the very athletes who had ended up at the black colleges would be ineligible for competetion. This meant that schools would have to provide nonathletic scholarships for poor blacks to attend classes but not to play, something that many of the traditional black colleges would be economically unable to do.

Competition was not the only point of contention for black educators and coaches. They insisted that the standardized SAT and ACT entrance

A Long Road to a Happy Ending

Although the story of Dean Tolson ended happily with his graduation from the University of Arkansas at the age of 36, it is filled with tribulation. Tolson was drafted by the Seattle Supersonics in 1974, cut in training camp, and picked up by the club after Christmas for the remainder of the season. He was released again in the fall of 1975, and he then went to the vaunted Eastern League where he toiled for $100 a game. Like a drowning swimmer, Tolson broke through the water again and played in '76 and '77 for the Supersonics. Finally, Tolson would tread the NBA waters no more, as the Sonics sent him packing in 1978. And pack he did—from Anchorage to Manila to Valencia, Venezuela, to Caracas to Athens and eventually home to Kansas City, where he was broke and bewildered. Seeing no other options, Tolson returned to Fayetteville, where he studied as much as 9 hours a day, retook his 38 hours of F, graduated, and during the entire time felt much frustration over his original bleak academic experience. These bleak academic experiences are what the proponents of Proposition 48 hoped to eliminate. (There is a flip side to the Tolson story that will be discussed in chapter 7.)

exams were biased against blacks, and they believed that they had the statistics to support their argument. Some black educators even went so far as to hint at a conspiracy to reduce the numbers and impact of black athletes in big-time intercollegiate athletics.

These protestations were largely ignored or dismissed, and minimum standards proponents constantly pointed out that the cutoff scores of 700 for the SAT and 15 for the ACT (now 18 with the enhanced scale) were extremely lenient and excluded only a fraction of all prospective students taking the exam. They also defended the new NCAA rules by advancing the argument that colleges and universities should not become farm systems for professional leagues, pervert the university mission by enrolling "dumb athletes," or exploit athletes by recruiting young men who had no chance of graduating.[18]

The Wide Swath of Prop 48

Despite all of the breastbeating and justification that accompanied support for the new academic standards, even the most ardent proponents were surprised by the impact of Proposition 48 and the degree to which it had taken its toll on black athletes. The initial year for the new rules, 1986, found nearly 400 incoming freshman athletes ineligible to compete in big-time football and basketball. This meant that nearly 10 percent of all freshman football players and 13 percent of all freshman players in men's basketball were affected by the new standards. These figures alone were not so shocking; it was the realization that the "overwhelming majority of the ineligible players" (nearly 85 percent) were black that caused a stir and seemed to confirm the suspicions of those who opposed the new standards.[19]

The trends did not abate, either. According to a 1989 NCAA study, 8.7 percent of "prospective student athletes" in men's basketball were partial qualifiers, with an astonishing 95 percent of this group being black. The figures for football were similar, with 9.6 percent of the incoming freshmen entering as partial qualifiers and blacks constituting 81 percent of the group. Granted, blacks did account for 46 percent of the total incoming freshman student-athletes surveyed,[20] but the 95 percent and 81 percent figures for basketball and football obviously indicate an inordinate black representation. It should also be noted that these figures are for partial qualifiers—prospective student-athletes with at least a 2.0 grade point average—and do not include exiting high school football and basketball players with cumulative GPAs below that level. Further, many black student-athletes are directed to junior colleges and never sign with Division I schools, and thus are excluded from the study.

The increased use of the junior college may be a primary reason for a leveling off of the *total* number of Proposition 48 victims (e.g., Division I men's basketball Proposition 48 recruits have dropped from a total of 162 in 1987 to 111 in 1988 and 105 in 1989).[21] Programs have become more selective, more careful, because the "wasting" of a scholarship on an unknown quantity is a risky venture in the tumultuous world of big-time athletics. Anyway, the slight decrease in the number of Proposition 48 partial qualifiers is hardly a sign that black athletes and their high schools are responding to the academic challenges set into motion by a committee of white college presidents.

Temple University coach John Chaney, an outspoken critic of Proposition 48, has equated the new NCAA measures with violations of civil rights law. Said Chaney, "They [the NCAA] are not above a civil-rights violation with both Prop 48 and Prop 42. You're talking about predominantly blacks. You're not talking about anyone else."[22]

Certainly, the comparatively large numbers of black athletes succumbing to the new minimum standards (see Table 6.1) would support Chaney's contentions. However, examining only the effects of Proposition 48 is no more sagacious than the shortsighted reasoning behind the legislation itself. A thorough look at the tests, the resulting penalties, and the apparent flaws in the Proposition 48 rationale is necessary for a true understanding of the situation.

The most controversial aspect of the Proposition 48 debate centers on the use of the ACT and SAT tests to determine a student-athlete's eligibility for athletic competition. Most people have no qualms about the re-

Table 6.1   Matriculation Rates of Division I Partial Qualifiers

176 Division I schools responded to the following NCAA survey question for men's revenue sports:

"To your knowledge, have prospective student-athletes who were partial qualifiers (i.e., those who earned overall grade-point averages of 2.000 or higher in high school and graduated but did not meet the core-curriculum grade-point average and/or test-score requirements) matriculated at your institution in the fall of 1989?"

| | Number not meeting | | | | | | | | |
| | Core GPA requirement | | | Test score requirement | | | Both requirements | | |
Group	Black	White	Other	Black	White	Other	Black	White	Other
Basketball	5	4	0	45	1	1	12	1	2
Football	19	3	1	135	21	7	42	5	2
Total	24	7	1	180	22	8	54	6	4

Source: *The NCAA News*, 21 February 1990.

quired 2.0 grade point average or the core curriculum of required high school course work, but many people, black educators in particular, feel that both of the widely used standardized tests are racially biased against blacks and other minorities often excluded from the American mainstream. The constant insistence on the tests' unfairness is not based on whimsy or suspicion. As David Owen says in the *Journal of Education*, "There is a considerable gap between the average SAT performance of whites and that of blacks, Mexican-Americans, and Puerto Ricans, and between people whose families have a lot of money and people whose families don't."[23] In fact, when the Proposition 48 standards were drawn up, the average score on the verbal SAT was "443 for whites and 339 for blacks. This gap has narrowed somewhat in the last five years, but a large difference still exists."[24] The esteemed members of the ACE Ad Hoc Committee had to be cognizant of these blatant differences between whites and blacks in standardized test performance, and it is this very point that has many people crying foul.

The utility and validity of a standardized admission test have always been subject to debate. Much has been made of the fact that Carl Campbell Brigham, the originator of the SAT, was a racist who expressed his remorse over the abolition of slavery. Although this may unfortunately be true, even Brigham recognized the limitations of his test and other standardized measures of intelligence and achievement. Said the so-called "father of the SAT" in the *New York Times*, on December 4th, 1938:

> The original and fallacious concept of the I.Q. was that it reported some mysterious attribute but now it is generally conceded that all tests are susceptible to training and to varying degrees of environmental opportunity. The tests measure a result and not its origin. Different types of tests will vary in their sensitivity to environmental opportunity, and it is ridiculous to claim that any test score is related to the germ plasm, and that alone.[25]

These are perceptive words from a man who at one point referred to the black race as a "sub-species."[26] His references to "training" and "environmental opportunity" probably point to the best explanations for the performance of a race he apparently scorned.

Poor Blacks and Testing

Why do blacks do poorly on standardized admission tests, and what relevance does this hold for the Proposition 48 controversy? Well, if blacks do systematically score lower because of generalizable and identifiable factors, and if these factors are largely beyond the control of a 17-year-old, then logic would demand a hard review of the Proposition 48 legislation and the consideration of its repeal. And the reality is that a good number of educators feel that this is just the case.

Reasons for Poor Performance

There are several reasons why a student might fare poorly on a standardized admission test, and a 1986 Iowa State University report specifically cited six:

- A student may be tired or ill and not functioning up to par.
- A student may suffer from a form of test anxiety.
- A student may be unprepared and not understand the test's directions.
- A student may be a slow worker and hurt by the timed nature of the test.
- A student may have a weak academic background.
- A student may not understand the concepts being tested.[27]

These difficulties could affect all students, and they are hardly exclusive to blacks. However, considering the academic status of blacks and other minorities who experience disproportionate poverty, it is obvious that many blacks and other low-income students would be severely hampered by some, if not all, of the six factors cited in the Iowa State report. It basically comes down to the same lack of experience and opportunity that hinders all disadvantaged children throughout their educations. Blacks score poorly on the SAT for the same reasons that black children have lower reading scores in elementary school; it is simply no great mystery. The enormous effect of poverty on academic achievement goes unnoticed only by people who refuse to look or who wish to avoid the real issues.

A classic example of this scenario is found in the results of a 1987 study by the Educational Testing Service (ETS) of Princeton, New Jersey, publishers of the SAT. Titled "Factors Affecting Differential Item Functioning for Black Examinees on Scholastic Aptitude Test Analogy Items," this 56-page study can be condensed into one simple point: "Black students need more time to complete the SAT verbal sections than do their white counterparts."[28] In other words, the deficient reading skills of black examinees cause them to score more poorly on the exam. As previously stated, blacks in general have weaker reading skills because more of them come from low-income backgrounds where experiences beneficial to early school achievement are fewer and opportunities for reading and access to books are less common. The experiences of the minority poor are different, and the language of the minority poor is different. It should therefore come as no shock that their scores on admission tests are different. Unfortunately, many ascribe the latter difference to an ability deficit.

Other theories have been posited to explain why blacks perform poorly on achievement tests, and they often center on motivation. A 1985 study investigated the possibility that black and white students do not use the same "measuring sticks" in the development of self-concept, and that scoring well on standardized tests may be more important to whites. Two possible explanations are cited by Rosemary Kellenberger:

> (1) "interpersonal mediation" or "reference group" theory, which states that persons compare themselves only with those with whom they identify; (2) "subcultural encapsulation" theory stating that groups can preserve positive self-images by adopting a "system blame" excuse to explain any low self-perceptions. Possibly what we are seeing here [black achievement] is some of this "system blame" rationalization which whites, having no group identification, are denied.[29]

All groups and individuals probably rationalize failures to a certain extent, but it is hard to believe that rationalization and copping out are not the results of the educational problems inherent in poverty instead of their causes. The fact is that most explanations come back to the point that many blacks and other minorities lack the basic skills and background to succeed on the SAT and ACT exams. The people on the ACE Ad Hoc Committee are very intelligent and highly educated. They know that an inordinate percentage of blacks exist in poverty and come from broken homes. They know that many blacks come of school age at an experiential disadvantage and attend inner-city elementary schools that are overcrowded and underfunded. They know that many black children acquire academic deficits early in their school careers that only increase with time. They know that many prospective black student-athletes from inner-city or impoverished rural areas will fail to meet the ACT and SAT cutoff scores they helped to set. Why, then, did they and do they continue to support the Proposition 48 requirements?

Accuracy of Standardized Tests as Predictors of Academic Success

According to Sheldon Hackney, University of Pennsylvania president and Ad Hoc Committee member, the legislated use of a standardized test is "controversial," but it is "the single best predictor of academic performance."[30]

Is Hackney's contention about the SAT and ACT tests' validity as accurate academic predictors a widely held belief? Apparently it is not. ETS President Gregory R. Anrig declared his opposition to Proposition 48 because it used the test ETS develops and administers, the SAT, in determining a cutoff score for ascertaining eligibility. Anrig's concerns are supported by research showing that admission tests alone are not the best predictors of college performance, and by a 1984 report in *The College Board Review* stating that "test publishers have consistently cautioned against the use of test scores alone for determining admission to college."[31]

Although skepticism from the president of the involved testing company and other statistically reliable sources would seemingly justify the questioning of Proposition 48's legitimacy, perhaps the strongest evidence in the case against the rule can be found in a 1987 report in the *Research Quarterly for Exercise and Sport*. From 1977 to 1983, all scholarship athletes entering the University of Michigan football program were identified and tracked throughout their college careers. The purpose of the study was to determine if three variables—SAT scores, high school grade point average, and high school rank—were equally valid predictors of college grade point average and/or graduation. During the 6-year period 162 subjects were studied, and the findings were startling as far as Proposition 48 is concerned.

The study revealed that SAT scores were unrelated to college grade point average for black athletes and were weakly related for nonblacks. In fact, high school grade point average alone predicted college grade point average for the black athlete. Accurate graduation rate prediction was also difficult to obtain from the three variables. For blacks, it was predicted nearly as well by high school grade point average as it was by college grade point average. However, high school grade point average was not a good predictor for the graduation rate of nonblacks, with SAT scores predicting only slightly better. The researchers concluded their study by writing, "For athletes, high school grade point average is the single best predictor of college success among predictors commonly used and is not improved by adding an aptitude measure."[32] They also conjectured that "Bylaw 5-1-(j) [Proposition 48] would fail to correct the problem of student exploitation and would have serious negative consequences for black athletes."[33]

It is curious that the Ad Hoc Committee's "best single predictor" could be so different from the Michigan study's "best single predictor." At the very least, a contradiction of this magnitude would appear to warrant a suspension of the Proposition 48 legislation until a consensus could be reached. The NCAA, however, has applied the opposite logic: Act first, study later. The effects of Proposition 48 will be analyzed at the end of its first 5 years.

Pennsylvania's Hackney is surely a wise man, and the Ad Hoc Committee is not a ship of fools. There is a certain amount of logic to their thinking. Adopting the tougher Prop 48 standards might indeed force the secondary schools to educate black athletes more adequately; and, obviously, someone earning an ACT score of 35 is probably better prepared for college than the unfortunate person scoring a 7. The problem, though, is that setting standards is not the same as offering solutions, and the differences in test scores are not always so clear-cut. The discrepancy between a nonqualifying 17 and a qualifying 18 is minimal at best, and it may not even be that when the errors of statistical measurement are considered. This seems a frivolous and careless way to make decisions, especially decisions that have such a powerful impact on the lives of talented youngsters.

Proposition 42

Despite the uncertainty and controversy surrounding Proposition 48, the NCAA doggedly plowed ahead, and in early 1989 the membership passed an amended version of Prop 48 commonly known as Proposition 42.[34] The amended legislation eliminated the so-called partial qualifier by mandating that prospective student-athletes not meeting both high school GPA and test score standards were ineligible for any form of financial aid from an NCAA institution. This resulted in low-income student-athletes' being denied access to Division I institutions solely on the basis of standardized test scores. For example, a student-athlete could have earned an overall high school GPA of 3.0 and have succeeded in the 11 core curriculum classes, but an ACT composite score of 14 or a 680 combined score on the SAT would prevent him from accepting a scholarship and sitting out his freshman season, as was the procedure under the original Proposition 48.

Consider the case of University of Michigan basketball player Rumeal Robinson. Robinson, the hero of Michigan's 1989 national championship title game victory, was a so-called Proposition 48 casualty because of low standardized test scores. He nevertheless enrolled at Michigan in the fall of 1986, where he received an athletic scholarship and was placed in an intensive tutorial program. The efforts were successful, and as of the spring of 1989, Robinson, who had been abandoned at age 10, was carrying a 2.9 grade point average and advancing toward a degree. If Proposition 42 had been in existence, Robinson could not have afforded to pay his way to the university, and he would have been forced to attend a junior college where some of the academic programs are dubious at best.[35]

Though the Robinson case is a success story under the guidelines set by Proposition 48, it should not be seen as evidence for its legitimacy. One worse grade in a high school class or one scheduling foul-up with his core classes, and Robinson might have been a nonqualifier under the rules as they then stood. As it was, he was prevented from practicing with the team by the NCAA's absurd logic that an athlete should not even be associated with the game until his academics are in order (as if Robinson never touched a basketball during his entire freshman year—a ridiculous supposition). In any case, Robinson's story and others notwithstanding, the adoption of the Proposition 42 legislation set off an immediate furor that was epitomized by the highly publicized and dramatic walkout by Georgetown coach John Thompson. Thompson vowed to continue his symbolic coaching boycott until the NCAA reviewed and acted on the Proposition 42 measure. Thompson, whose actions received much support and sympathy, won out. After a meeting in Kansas City between the coach, NCAA leaders, and Georgetown University administrators, application of the rule was postponed, and it was eventually rescinded at the 1990 NCAA Convention.

The rationale of Proposition 48 and the related and rescinded Proposition 42 merely reflected the much-talked-about educational reform movement that swept the nation during the same period. Not based on sound statistical research, and adopted against the urgings of erudite educators in the field of testing, Proposition 48 was—and is—just another superficial fix to a problem with no simple solutions. Its logic is unsound, and it embodies the many shortcomings of so much of the early 1980s' education reform legislation. Harold L. Hodgkinson of The Institute for Educational Leadership spoke indirectly to the NCAA situation when he wrote:

We also discovered a widespread concern that the current spate of state-based reform legislation will only increase the group of push-outs to be added to the drop-outs. Eliminating low performers from the public schools was seen as a way of displacing the problem, not solving it. Out of school, these students present more of a social and economic problem than they do IN school.[36]

Certainly, universities and colleges do not serve the same function as the nation's public elementary, junior high, and high schools, but Hodgkinson's point should not be ignored. So much of the reform has essentially consisted of denying opportunity rather than initiating meaningful change in the conditions that are the root of the problem. Wrote Thomas Harper, regional superintendent of the District of Columbia Public Schools:

> Minimum academic standards have been with us a long time, but have not been strictly enforced or monitored, primarily because they are virtually impossible to standardize. If we are going to make a difference, every effort should be made to improve student achievement and teacher performance—not just for those who participate in activities.[37]

Not a Solution

Proposition 48 neither addresses nor provides solutions to the problems of academic achievement, and the notion of methodological reform is not remotely considered. The legislation assumes that suddenly student-athletes, primarily blacks, are going to "wake up," change their priorities, and make startling gains in their academic achievements. How this will happen is uncertain, but NCAA logic assumes that the behavioristic, outcome-oriented rule will be the source of a great scholastic transition. Cause and effect are not always so clear-cut, though, and the NCAA and its policy leaders may have missed the boat on this issue. History shows that it is never easy to legislate change. With all of the statistical and logical contradictions inherent in the minimum standards position, it would appear that Proposition 48 lacked adequate forethought and should be repealed or suspended until further study. As was reported in the Spring 1984 College Board Review, "There exists no research which would indicate that stopping a student from participating in athletics will, in turn, engender improved academic performance."[38] Finally, if the powers that be are concerned about the pressures of athletic competition during a student-athlete's freshman year, why don't they simply declare freshmen ineligible for varsity game competition? Many, including myself, have advocated this, and it would end the unfair filtering process now used by making Proposition 48 moot.

Additional Reform Efforts

The NCAA is considering or has considered other legislation related to academic performance.

Academic Progress Requirements

A 1988 proposal to stiffen requirements for satisfactory academic progress was initially passed and then overturned for reconsideration by the NCAA convention delegates. As described earlier in the section on graduation rates, the amendment would require student-athletes to earn a grade point average of 1.600 after their initial season of competition, 1.800 after their second year, and 2.000 after completion of their third year of competition.[39] Placed before the assembly by the Presidents Commission, the proposal met with bitter opposition from institutions that viewed the new standards as favoring student-athletes majoring in less taxing disciplines and universities offering watered-down programs. The legislation is currently tabled, although there is speculation that an amended version will be reintroduced at the 1991 NCAA Convention. In addition, the privately funded Knight Commission, a 2-year, $2 million project, is studying the feasibility of having the NCAA add "a successively greater minimum accumulative grade-point average to the satisfactory-progress legislation."[40] The findings of the national blue-ribbon panel are expected in the spring of 1991.

Availability of Graduation Rate Data

Another addition to the thick *NCAA Manual* is legislation requiring institutions to make graduation rate data available in the recruiting process. Introduced by the Presidents Commission at the 1990 NCAA Convention, the procedures require disclosure of Division I and Division II programs' graduation figures according to sport, race, and sex. The rapidity with which this legislation was passed and the fact that it met little opposition are indicative of the NCAA's attempt to forestall federal involvement in this area. However, the collegians failed to beat the legislators to the punch.

The "Student's Right-To-Know Act" would require colleges and universities that receive federal aid to disclose the graduation rates of student-athletes and of students at large. Originally sponsored by Senator Bill Bradley (Democrat, New Jersey), Representative Tom McMillen (Democrat, Maryland), and Representative Ed Towns (Democrat, New York), the measure has passed in the Senate and will probably pass in the House. The graduation data, provided to the Department of Education, would be broken down by sport, race, sex, and field of study.[41] Bradley claims the legislation is necessary "to restore the balance between athletics and academics." He adds that "too many student-athletes sacrifice academic achievement to the fantasy of professional sports. Only one of 10,000 high school athletes who wants a career in professional sports ever realizes that aspiration."[42]

The House and Senate measures have widespread support, but they have also been opposed by those citing government intrusion into intercollegiate athletics and "increased paperwork burdens."[43] The intrusion factor is what spurred the NCAA to pass its own similar legislation, and there is little doubt that the association would rather police itself in the graduation rate area.

What change will the federal bills or the NCAA legislation bring about? Certainly, prospective students and student-athletes have the right to know a particular institution's graduation rate, but what exactly will the information mean? The fact that one institution graduates 60 percent of its athletes and another graduates only 40 percent means little in itself. There are many variables involved, particularly the quality and integrity of the awarded degree, and it would be erroneous to read too much into a few simple percentages. Moreover, a negative result of the graduation rate reporting requirement would be the temptation to "ensure" the graduation of a school's student-athletes. This is already occurring to a certain degree with the aforementioned advent of bogus degree programs at some institutions.

Graduation Insurance

Consider the case of former University of Missouri and Indiana Pacer player Steve Stiponavich. A ruined knee ended Stiponavich's NBA career, and he was biding time in his hometown of St. Louis when he was interviewed by Jack Etkin of the *Kansas City Star*. When asked about his academic career, Stiponavich replied, "I took two correspondence courses last year and graduated in December. The diploma, they said, would be in the mail in February. I'm anxious to see it because I don't know what my major is. But I do have a four-year degree; I do know that." Indeed, he does!

Source: "Freak Condition Halts NBA Career." *Kansas City Star*, 4 February 1990, Sports-1.

If graduation rates became a primary and highly publicized recruiting factor, many institutions might see miraculous increases overnight in the graduation rates of their athletes, and many more "mystery degrees" might be awarded. Such outcomes can hardly be the intent of either the federal or the NCAA legislation, and they would only exacerbate the problem rather than solve it.

Academic Support Programs

Added to the various committees, bills, forums, proposals, and studies on the plight of academics in intercollegiate athletics are efforts of the institutions themselves to alleviate the problem through special academic support. As of 1986, approximately 55 percent of all Division I institutions offered some type of academic support system to their student-athletes.[44] These programs range from comprehensive approaches forming veritable campus departments to a single full- or part-time adviser who may be responsible only for the members of a single team. Support programs are sometimes affiliated with campus-wide study skills or remediation centers, but more often than not, they are a branch of the athletic department and are funded from athletic revenues. Veteran, degreed education professionals may staff a well-established, highly funded program, or a single graduate assistant may be inundated by the needs of an unmanageable number of athletes. Some programs have their own facilities—including computer labs or resource rooms—in athletic department offices or athletic dorms, whereas the facilities of others may be located in a solitary briefcase. Still, despite their differences, academic support programs for athletes have some common denominators, and the academic advisers or coordinators are constantly faced with the same dilemmas.

Academic Advisers

The academic adviser for athletes is a new entity that has come into existence as the pressures to win have caused football and basketball programs to recruit more and more student-athletes who are inadequately prepared for college-level academic work. Most of these advisers are between 31 and 40 years old, have been employed in their current positions for less than 5 years, hold master's or doctoral degrees, and have no coaching experience.[45] Their salaries average between $26,000 and $30,000, and they are responsible for budgets ranging from $7,000 to $333,000, with tutoring expenditures representing from $1,000 to $200,000 of that total. Their major responsibilities are serving *men's* athletic programs by doing academic monitoring, providing a liaison between athletic departments and academic faculties, counseling student-athletes, coordinating tutorial programs, supervising study halls for athletes, and sometimes recruiting.[46] But statistics such as these offer only a glimpse of the advisers' situations. They are often caught in a no-man's-land between the academic and the athletic—not jock enough or coach enough to have real power in the athletic department, and viewed with suspicion by the faculty as someone tainted by the athletic monster. It is a difficult and often untenable position from which to operate, and the troubles are compounded by student-athletes who choose not to make an effort academically or simply do not know how.

Perhaps the single greatest source of pressure for the academic adviser is the necessity of keeping key players eligible. The eligibility goal is the crux of the position. Some institutions may use lofty-sounding goals and philosophies to describe their academic support programs (the University of Missouri, for instance, has the Total Person Program), but keeping talented players on the field to keep the turnstiles turning is the true objective. Unfortunately, those who sometimes spin the turnstiles best, the urban blacks of the North and the rural blacks of the South, are frequently the least equipped to consistently maintain eligibility.

Herein lies the major problem for the academic adviser. What is practical may not always be ethical, and how can those two concerns be balanced—or should they be? Here is an illustration. Ballplayer X has 1 year of eligibility remaining after completion of his junior season. However, Ballplayer X passed only 6 credit hours in the fall semester, and he needs to earn 18 hours in spring and/or summer to remain eligible for next fall's action. The adviser's dilemma is this: X is struggling badly in his upper-division degree program course work; but according to NCAA rules, X should have a declared major by his junior year, and his course work should reflect progress toward a degree. Therefore, to enroll X in 18 hours of Mickey Mouse 101 would be a technical violation of the rules, and as the adviser knows, would not benefit X as a person, anyway. On the other hand, unless X takes the 18 hours of Mickey Mouse 101, he will probably flunk out and lose his senior season of eligibility. So what does the academic adviser do? Rationalizes! In the big picture of life, the rationalization goes, X is better off remaining in school than going home (probably true in many instances), whereas flunking out will definitely close the door to any slim opportunity for X to improve as a student and a person. Also, there is the matter of employment to consider: A Ballplayer X or two missing a much-anticipated senior season will result in the academic adviser's seeking job opportunities elsewhere. But here is the kicker. X may *expect* to gain his eligibility, and he may very well feel that the academic adviser is obligated to ensure it. X may or may not want to meet the adviser or his instructors halfway; he may simply believe that his athletic abilities and contributions will allow him to proceed academically at his own leisurely pace.

This scenario is more than common for those involved in academic support work. It is an everyday reality that is most difficult to cope with. Ann Mayo, athletic academic consultant for the University of Nevada, Las Vegas, believes that those involved in helping student-athletes with their academic work must follow a code of ethics to prevent such instances of academic advisement misconduct as blatant disregard for

NCAA, conference, or institutional rules; sexual relationships between advisers and student-athletes; "bartering" for grades with cash payments or season tickets; professional neglect; racial and/or sexual prejudice; and advisement that ultimately is more concerned with athletic eligibility than with a student-athlete's academic interests or life goals.[47] Said Mayo, "A code of professional ethics requires that we operate basically from a sense of 'fairness' and that we practice without distortion to fit the needs of any one person's point of view, be it the coach, the student-athlete, or ourselves."[48]

While Mayo's assertions are lined with worth and goodness, they fail to provide an adequate shelter from the harsh, pragmatic realities academic advisers must endure. Certainly, the academic well-being of the student-athlete should be the primary focus of an academic support system, but like an idealistic politician, the adviser must pay attention to the one who butters the bread. Academic advisers who show little concern for eligibility will soon find themselves in situations where they are unable to provide help for anyone.

Even in the purest of situations, academic support personnel may have difficulty establishing the rapport they need to relate meaningfully with the players. Most student-athletes understand that the head coach holds the purse—the athletic scholarship—and that class instructors hold the key—the grades required for eligibility. Academic advisers may be viewed as shadowy advocates who can indirectly help make life a little more pleasant (or unpleasant), but they are rarely afforded the respect that would allow them to facilitate the student-athlete's growth in academic disciplines and specific skill areas. Undoubtedly, some academic advisers are given the authority by head coaches or athletic directors to direct and discipline, but in other situations, only the most motivated of players and the most dedicated of advisers will work together to realize tangible gains.

The ambivalence of the student-athlete toward the academic adviser was illuminated by a 1983 Kansas State University study. In examining the "Significant Others" of college football players, researchers found that only 35 percent of those surveyed perceived the "Athletic Academic Counselor" as a positive influence. This compares to a 95 percent rating for certain teachers and 50 percent and 45 percent ratings for position coaches and the head coach, respectively. Of those included in the survey, 10 percent saw the "Athletic Academic Counselor" as a "negative influence," a figure lagging behind only the 15 percent negative rating of some poorly regarded teammates.[49] Global conclusions cannot be drawn from one isolated and somewhat dated dab of research, but that small amount of evidence combines with the obvious to paint a frustrating portrait of the tasks of academic advisers.

In spite of the peculiar obstacles facing academic support systems for athletes, they are a step in the right direction. If nothing else, the expen-

---

A Tough Row to Hoe

Consider the case of Ed Mooney, who became Baylor University's first athletic academic adviser in 1984. Mooney publicly expressed his frustration in the *Dallas Morning News* when he commented,

> We're just not getting the support collectively from everyone. In this job, you have to have a tremendous amount of support. One of the things is that when you're doing a good job, everyone tends to back off. But you need cooperation. When it starts to slide, you know it's time to leave.[a]

Mooney left in 1987. More blunt was Dale Pitts, Texas Christian University academic adviser. A former coach, principal, superintendent, and FBI agent, Pitts claimed that advising TCU student-athletes had been his most difficult job. Said Pitts:

> You've got two bosses and you can never completely satisfy either one. You try to do what the coaches want you to do, and the faculty gets mad. You do what the faculty wants and the coaches get mad. You do your best to stay on the fence, but someone's going to be mad.

Note. [a] Kevin Sherrington, "The Toughest Job . . .," *Dallas Morning News*, 29 June 1987, 1-B, 11-B.

---

diture of athletic revenues in the academic realm shows a modicum of progress. Of course, some critics contend that the programs' emphasis on eligibility shows their true exploitative colors, but it would be hard to contend that helping student-athletes in their course work does not at least have a few benefits. There have been documented successes, also. Georgetown, Notre Dame, and Northwestern are academically proud institutions that have received public acclaim for their academic support programs. Every weeknight at Northwestern, athletes from all 17 varsity sports assemble from 7 to 10 p.m., and graduate assistants and staff tutors offer assistance in all subjects. Georgetown's success in assisting Patrick Ewing and other minority basketball players with their academic work has provided Hoya Coach John Thompson with the credibility necessary to speak out on such controversial academic issues as Proposition 42.[50]

Increasing Study Time

Other less publicized institutions have also achieved positive results. The North Texas State University athletic department, with help from the

NTSU School of Community Service and the school's Center for Behavioral Studies, developed a unique contingency management system to increase the time student-athletes spent actually studying. Implemented within the framework of the athletic study hall for students whose grade point averages were mostly below 2.0, the system rewarded those who diligently remained on task with an early dismissal from study hall (e.g., after 1-1/2 hours instead of 2 hours). This contingency repeatedly proved effective, with on-task behavior occupying from 93 percent to 100 percent of participants' time during required study hall hours. This compares to preprogram figures that "rarely were above 70 percent."[51]

Here at Southwest Missouri State University we have also experienced a certain degree of success. Our program, originally implemented with the men's basketball team, was loosely based on intervention strategies involving a heavy dose of individual accountability and responsibility. Players who performed well in the classroom received the respect and responsibility accorded any successful adult, and they were encouraged to take the lead in determining their own academic destinies. Conversely, players whose classroom performance was unsatisfactory were required to attend nightly study halls where self-reliance was emphasized instead of a heavy use of tutors. In 2 years, the team's semester GPA rose from a mediocre 2.05 to a significantly stronger 2.68. The program has now been expanded to the entire athletic department, and our graduation rates are slowly but surely rising.

Tutorial Programs

One final example of an academic support program that reaped positive benefits was a Lynchburg, Virginia, high school endeavor. Although collegiate and high school athletic programs differ significantly, they both harbor distractions that interfere with the academic advancement of student-athletes. To address this problem, the Lynchburg Public Schools developed an athletic study hall for all students "who did not have a 2.0 for the previous semester."[52] The study hall met for 1 hour at the end of the regular school day and was staffed by teachers who served as volunteer tutors. Each athlete attended an individualized conference "emphasizing the reasons for the study hall and the expectations that we had of athletes who were there."[53] Attendance was mandatory, and excessive absences resulted in expulsion from the team. The study hall program had positive results. More than 30 percent of its participants earned 2.0 grade point averages, and more than 50 percent earned their "highest-ever" GPAs. Failing grades were decreased significantly. The Lynchburg study hall program was deemed a success by all who were involved.

Although the Lynchburg Public Schools demonstrated success with the tutorial facet of their study hall program, and though tutoring is heavily utilized by many Division I athletic departments, an overreliance on tutorial relationships may prove disappointing. Tutoring can undercut a student-athlete's sense of responsibility for his learning by placing the tutor in the position of primary responsibility. In other words, a player may come to see his tutor as an automatic free ticket to academic success. When this happens, the onus of responsibility for class work shifts from the player to the tutor, and the wrong person ends up performing most of the required tasks. Such a situation is not only detrimental to the educational growth of the player, but it is unethical as well: One may well question whose work it is. Precautions must be taken to establish guidelines for tutorial sessions, or some players' sense of responsibility for their scholastic work will continue to erode.

Not only can tutorial programs stunt the development of student-athletes' academic responsibility, but they can also give a false sense of security to academic advisers and coaches in charge of administrating support programs. This happens all too often in many Division I programs, where tutoring constitutes the bulk of the academic support activities. There may be an erroneous feeling of a job well done as scholarly pairs perform academic pirouettes, and many coaches and counselors shake their heads in collective wonder when the inevitable failing grades come rolling in.

Perhaps the sometimes disappointing results of tutorial programs can be traced to a lack of commitment or expertise on the part of the athletes or tutors, but quite frequently, they are the product of disorganization and a curious lack of involvement on the part of the coordinator. Sometimes, even the tutorial programs themselves are corrupt. Bret Iba, a former assistant coach at the University of New Orleans and the University of Idaho, currently at Southwest Missouri State University, tells of a program described to him by a colleague:

> The assistant coach was in his first year with a program at a new institution. He was going through the previous year's tutorial records, and they showed an incredible number of contact hours and exorbitant expenditures. He finally called in a returning team member to ask him about the situation. After several minutes of questioning, the player finally admitted that the time cards had been doctored. The tutors then "kicked back" the overpayments to the players they had been tutoring. In other words, someone had concocted a nifty little illegal payment scheme.

Few tutorial programs are fronts for irregular activities. Some are merely exercises in futility. One former graduate assistant at a Southeastern Conference institution called his school's tutorial program "a three-ring circus with the tutors, players, and coaches running amok with no apparent direction. The entire academic program was in disarray."

Unfortunate situations like those described by the graduate assistant and Coach Iba (grandson of the legendary Henry Iba) are not necessarily the fault of any single person. When authority is delegated, as it is when a tutor is assigned to an athlete, there is a natural tendency to assume that progress is being made. Unfortunately, this may not be the case. The tutor-as-savior philosophy should be viewed with caution by those who work with student-athletes.

A comprehensive and holistic approach to an academic support program that includes the integrated efforts of advisers, coaches, tutors, and the student-athletes themselves would be the ideal way to attack the academic problems inherent in Division I athletics. "Teamwork, discipline, cooperation, time management, organization, pride in ability," and other positive traits derived from sports participation can be "transferred to the student's academic repertoire."[54] This would require patience, effort, and nurturing, but the end results might be well worth it. Said Rosemary Thompson, an assistant principal at Oscar Frommel Smith High School in Chesapeake, Virginia, "A comprehensive program to enhance the academic potential of student athletes could fuse a relationship between sports participation and career goals."[55] Of course, such an effort would necessitate the allocation of more resources. But if the presidents and athletic administrators are as serious about improving academics as they claim to be, they should hardly be timid about spearheading such a movement. Anyway, the ball is already rolling, and academic support systems to improve the lives of individual student-athletes, systems financed by the revenues earned from their performances, are among the more sane and logical reform efforts that have been initiated.

CHAPTER 7

A Few Sensible Suggestions

Division I athletics will not undergo an immediate transformation into an activity that is pure and holy. There will not even be a backing off period where the involved parties examine and assess, with athletics reemerging from a butterfly-like metamorphosis. Instead, big-time intercollegiate sports will keep plodding along doing good and doing ill, and any changes will have to occur midstream. Positive signs are appearing, though. The NCAA, with its veritable war chest of revenues, is finally cracking down on the cheaters. Kentucky, Oklahoma, Kansas, Florida, and other major programs have all been severely penalized for a wide variety of unsavory transgressions. The message is now clear: The organization is finally ready to police itself, and no institution will be immune to investigation or sanctions. Academic progress is also being made. Although some ideas and projects such as Propositions 48 and 42 were hurriedly adopted and were not based on sound and logical reasoning, the mere presence of dialogue on the topic can only signal an improvement over the sorry mess that previously existed. Various proposals to improve the college games have emerged from diverse segments of society, and their future implementation could ensure the realization of the wonderful opportunities that intercollegiate athletics can ultimately provide.

Removing the Worm From the Apple

Many suggestions have been offered regarding the NCAA's efforts to clean up the academic pond scum that has consistently washed ashore. Some recommendations, such as one that athletic programs lose scholarships for each player who fails to graduate within 5 years,[1] are ludicrous and unenforceable. As has been stated before, legislating graduation rates may result in players' "graduating" whether they should or not. This would only add another problematic dimension to an issue not needing further complication. Some proposals have been excellent, however, and their primary components have been assimilated in a group of concrete recommendations discussed later in this chapter.

Representative Thomas A. Luken of Ohio, who in 1987 "drafted legislation to establish an impartial advisory commission under Congressional aegis" for college athletics, has proposed several reforms that he believes would greatly improve the academic-athletic relationship in Division I sports:

(1) Athletic departments should be integrated into the universities, rather than being separate corporations with separate budgets and independent goals.

(2) Student athletes should be integrated with other students, eliminating all separate team housing.

(3) The length of basketball and football seasons should be shortened, with a reduced number of games and shorter practice seasons.

(4) Freshmen should not be eligible for varsity play. Athletes should have the first year to get acclimated on campus as students.

(5) Academic standards should be tightened. "Academic progress" should be clearly defined to keep student athletes on track for graduation with other members of their class.[2]

Luken's reforms are on target, although monitoring standardized "academic progress" could lead to many of the problems previously associated with legislating academics. Reviewing a transcript to make certain a student-athlete has passed his 24 hours is one thing, but ascertaining progress toward a communications degree at one institution or a general studies degree at another is something entirely different. Luken's contention that athletes should be making legitimate efforts to earn degrees is most valid, but enforcing such a reform may prove to be impractical.

It has been suggested that if an athlete holds up his end of the contractual agreement by staying in school and playing all 4 years that he is eligible, the institution should then be obligated to finance his degree studies for whatever amount of time was necessary—as long as the student-athlete was enrolled in a degree program, going to class, and attending to his studies. It has also been proposed that a student-athlete be allowed to complete his education at "a comparable academic program near his home," with his original institution paying for tuition. Wrote Steve Robinson,

> Sounds like a lot for schools to cope with, especially in these days of rising costs. All the more reason the proposed contract makes sense. If colleges shudder at the thought of footing the bill for their former athletes for years on end, then let them educate their athletes properly the first time around.[3]

Robinson's notion may seem radical, but if the exploitation of the student-athlete is a problem (and I believe it certainly is), then the idea definitely has merit. Anyway, Robinson is a writer, and writers can basically think in any way they like. University presidents are not so fortunate.

University of Iowa president Dr. Hunter Rawlings felt the wrath one can incur when he suggested that the NCAA ban freshmen from varsity competition. Rawlings even went so far as to say that if the NCAA did not adopt such a rule change, the University of Iowa would do so on its own within 3 years. Iowans were furious with the Rawlings proposal, as well as with other statements he made regarding athletics, and he was verbally attacked by everybody from head football coach Hayden Fry to Iowa governor Terry Branstad. Although freshman ineligibility is not a particularly wild-eyed idea—it used to be the norm—the response to Rawlings's suggestion illustrates the difficulty of enacting any meaningful reforms.

The Testing Quagmire

Although radical changes in the way the NCAA and the athletic departments of its member institutions deal with the academics of student-athletes cannot be implemented overnight, there is one area in which the NCAA could and should quickly heed the advice of some sagacious individuals. This area is standardized testing and its use by the NCAA to determine a student-athlete's initial eligibility. As previously discussed, not only is the use of SAT and ACT scores unfair to minority athletes from low-income socioeconomic backgrounds, but the very premise underlying their use may be faulty. Donald Stewart, president of the College Board, announced that he was shocked when he heard about the NCAA's Proposition 48 ruling. Stewart was paraphrased as claiming that "no single test should have such power."[4] Many people, including me, support Georgetown coach John Thompson's assertion that eligibility should be based on high school grade point average and the core curriculum requirement.

If the NCAA and the powerful Presidents Commission stubbornly persist in using minimum SAT and ACT scores as eligibility cutoff points, the NCAA should take some of its millions of dollars in revenues and provide test-taking workshops for prospective student-athletes. These workshops could be conducted regionally on the campuses of member institutions. The likely beneficiaries could be identified as those who had failed in their first attempt at the ACT or SAT and who had already signed with a member institution.

Obviously, a widely offered workshop to improve the test-taking skills of prospective minority student-athletes would be a logistic and administrative nightmare. But if the NCAA is to adhere to its present Proposition 48 guidelines, it should be compelled to take all precautions to negate bias or discrimination. Of course, it would be simpler and better to suspend the Proposition 48 regulations because, as Father Timothy Healy, president of Georgetown, once said, "No test can tell you how much fire is in anyone's belly."[5]

Helping the Black Student-Athlete

Regardless of NCAA regulations and the varying academic programs offered to different institutions' student-athletes, the colleges have an obligation to act responsibly in the education of black athletes. This obligation is predicated not only on the unfortunate educational status of blacks and other American minorities, but also on the fact that many black student-athletes are plucked out of environments completely foreign to the collegiate world and will inevitably struggle without care and help. Growing up in an inner-city broken home where drugs and violence may be a way of life is hardly the equivalent of attending prep school, and "colleges that recruit such youngsters and expose them to severe culture shock bear a special responsibility to provide discipline and educational opportunity."[6]

Helping poor black students focus on their studies and attain academic goals may not be an easy task. The difficulty is due in part to the harsh economic realities facing the poor black community and the persistent myth that professional athletics may be a legitimate and feasible means of escape. As Tulane University history professor Lawrence N. Powell stated in a 1989 issue of Newsweek, "We've abandoned the poor black community, and they've become isolated as middle-class blacks move out. All they're left with is no jobs or McJobs. Never have these kids had more pressure to perform athletically."[7]

Unfortunately, the intense recruitment of young black athletes only perpetuates and glorifies the pro myth and heightens the pressure to concentrate solely on the athletic endeavor. If for no other reason than this, Division I institutions should do everything they can do to soundly educate their minority student-athletes. But there is another issue here, as well: that of higher education's obligation to society as a whole. When one considers the fact that by the year 2000 one of every three Americans will be nonwhite,[8] the collegiate commitment to the minority student-athlete becomes even more important.

Advice to improve the academic status of the student-athlete has not been focused only on the NCAA or its member institutions. The role of the athletes and their families, particularly black athletes and *their* families, has also been addressed. Some critics find that black families are far too preoccupied with sports and the media's portrayal of professional sports as a high-prestige occupation. A UCLA study found that black families "are four times more likely than white families to view their children's involvement in athletics as something that may lead to a professional sports career."[9]

John Hammond, assistant basketball coach for the Los Angeles Clippers and a former assistant coach at the University of Nebraska, Houston Baptist University, and Southwest Missouri State, reiterated similar findings from his own personal experience. Hammond, who is white, spoke of a disturbing visit he once had with a black player's father at a summer league playground game between the player's junior and senior collegiate years. The player, a fine student who graduated in 4 years, had started the previous season because of his intelligence and outstanding effort. However, he stood only 5'10" and rarely made a jumper (a generous description of the player's awkward shot) from beyond 15 feet. These are hardly qualifications for the NBA, but the player's father, a bright and respected businessman in his community, was convinced that his son would soon be taking Magic Johnson to the hole in some future playoff tilt. The assistant coach was flabbergasted at the father's expectations, and he finally surmised that so ingrained was the pro myth in the black consciousness that not even a man as thoughtful as the player's father could see the forest through the trees.

Harry Edwards agreed with Coach Hammond when he explained, "The already heightened black emphasis upon sports achievement that is fostered through myths, stereotypes, family and community attitudes, and the media is further intensified by black youths' early educational and athletic experiences."[10] Edwards feels that, in large part, the academic problems of black student-athletes cannot be solved on the college campuses but must be confronted in the black home.[11] This is exactly the point stated earlier in this book: The limited opportunities and experiences associated with low-income minority families are the ultimate cause of the academic-athletic contradictions facing so many black players. Unfortunately, mere effort on the part of poor black parents may not be enough to leap the tremendous economic hurdles they face. But Edwards's contention that black parents "must instill black youths with values stressing the priority of educational achievement over athletic participation and even proficiency"[12] points out an excellent place to begin.

Other black educators have also emphasized the necessity for the entire black community to accept responsibility for the education of its children. Reginald Wilson presented a paper at the 1986 annual meeting of the National Alliance of Black School Educators that illuminated the educational and economic crises currently facing black and Hispanic Americans. Wilson stressed that the "viability of this nation as a participant in the global economy" was dependent on finding solutions to current problems. Wilson spoke directly to the black community with the following statement:

> We must reengage the tie between the black middle class and the black lower class. Not only are we distanced physically by many of us living in the suburbs, and like our white colleagues, coming in the city in the morning and leaving in the afternoon, but many of us are increasingly psychologically distant. I don't say that to make anyone feel guilty, only to state a fact that we do not have the strong communal and economic ties and organizations like the Asians or Jews that bind the group together *irrespective* of where they live or what economic class they belong to.[13]

Those who like to believe that racial issues are a thing of the past may not like the tone of Wilson's statement. But if college athletic scholarship opportunities do provide greater access to a college education for many black youths, the black community must seize the initiative and make sure the chance is not squandered.

Finally, it is not enough for blacks and minorities to accept increased responsibility for the education of their youth. There has to be a commitment from individuals—the student-athletes—to persevere at higher education. Minority student-athletes need to be helped "to assume responsibility for their studies and regard education as their most important priority and their passport to economic and social mobility."[14] Simply stated, black athletes cannot allow the wide array of readily available excuses and cop-outs to undermine their excellent chance to obtain a college education. I believe the NCAA could enact one very simple rule that might help in this area. The NCAA should require every prospective student-athlete to sign a disclaimer that acknowledges his slim chances of turning professional in his sport. This might not solve the problem completely, but it would counteract much of the hogwash a recruit hears during the recruiting process. Perhaps, along the same lines, every student who signs a letter of intent could be mailed Richard E. Lapchick's guide for student-athletes, *On the Mark*. Compiled at the Northeastern University Center for the Study of Sport in Society, the book gives excellent and simple advice on avoiding the many pitfalls often encountered by student-athletes. Although these two simple and affordable suggestions are hardly panaceas, they at least represent doing the right thing.

A Few Simple Suggestions

Implementing all of the previous suggestions may not be feasible, as some of them probably border on wishful thinking. Still, the NCAA and the athletic programs of Division I institutions should consider their merit and begin initiating some of the proposed reforms, after taking into account the information presented here on the individual, institutional, and societal variables that affect college athletics and the academic progress of its participants. With both the recommendations and the realities of the situation in mind, those responsible could institute several specific and feasible reforms.

Work With the Public Schools

At the most basic level, the academic problems facing intercollegiate athletics are those plaguing the American educational system as a whole. Literacy and basic skills for the poor and minorities, appropriate educational goals for an evolving economy, sensible and· fair testing procedures, the formulation of adequate exit standards, the redressing of funding inequities, and the retention of students themselves are broad issues with which all educators must grapple. As long as such problems exist at the public school level, NCAA institutions will continue to face academic-athletic dilemmas.

Of course, the educational welfare of an entire nation may be beyond the scope of the NCAA and its member organizations, but there is no reason the group cannot be a powerful figurehead for the educational rights of all. The NCAA has already unleashed massive public relations campaigns concerning drug abuse and its own academic integrity. There is no reason this cannot be carried a step further, especially considering the fact that an educated and literate citizenry is the best protection the NCAA could have against the drug problems and scholastic faux pas that have plagued the organization in recent years. Minimally, each member institution should try to join a cooperative effort to ensure educational opportunity for all Americans. Such a commitment would be more than symbolic: It would foster a group mind-set that would deem unacceptable the inequities of the present educational system. Here are several specific suggestions:

- Continue drug awareness campaigns.

- Explore the feasibility of work-study programs in which student-athletes could serve as volunteers or role models in the public schools.
- Encourage member institutions to initiate youth literacy programs in their communities.
- Bring low-income youths onto campuses for positive interaction with student-athletes, faculty, and coaches.

These easily implemented ideas would not solve all of the country's problems, but they would be tangible acts that could only have positive outcomes.

Change the Distribution of Revenue

The NCAA's current method of distributing revenue from national tourneys, television and radio rights, and football bowl games is a primary source of many of the organization's current problems. The notion that an amateur athletic association doles out money according to who the winners are is contradictory, illogical, and absurd. The policy of paying teams and conferences for their on-the-field proficiency is a brand of shameless professionalism that encourages cheating and the downplaying of academics. It is little wonder that coaches or programs cheat when winning may mean hundreds of thousands of dollars added to a program's coffers. Of course, most Division I conferences have revenue-sharing programs, and there is nothing wrong with reaping rewards for a job well done. However, for the NCAA to maintain that players may not receive money for playing and then to turn around and monetarily reward the institutions and their programs for those players' performances is blatant hypocrisy.

Many would argue that an equitable distribution of NCAA moneys, with all member institutions sharing like amounts, would be unfair to the institutions that risk the most and provide the quality of entertainment that allows the NCAA and bowl games to pay out millions to the lucky participants. But those enjoying the current monopoly would have little to fear. Only moneys earned in national, organizationally sponsored events such as bowl games or the Final Four and NCAA-bargained television rights should be equally distributed. The thought that Alabama's budget would suddenly be brought down to the level of Middle Tennessee's is pure nonsense. Alabama still has all the advantages and most of the cards: a big-time conference with its own television contract for basketball, an average football attendance of 60,000 plus fans per game, a megadonor program for athletics, a huge statewide radio network that reaps advertising dollars. Middle Tennessee would still be a veritable peon in comparison to the Alabamas of the world. However, if all Division I schools received an equal share of the pie, there would be less pressure to participate in unethical activities because winning would not have the enormous financial consequences it currently does. Ultimately, the true beneficiaries of such a policy would be the student-athletes, whose welfare suffers when programs stray from the prudent course.

Deep down, everyone knows that the current payoff system is the root of most evil in intercollegiate athletics. And more and more coaches, athletic administrators, and university presidents are finally admitting it. Naturally, there will always be a scoundrel or two who will cheat the rules and his players' academics for an advantage regardless of the financial situation, but the pressure to keep victorious scoundrels around would lessen if winning were not synonymous with garnering NCAA-distributed moneys. Winning will always yield its profits in ticket sales and private support for an institution, but the NCAA should not reinforce this mentality. An amateur is one who does something for pleasure, not for pay. While pure amateurism for Division I athletics may be impossible to achieve, the NCAA should still conduct itself in an idealistic manner and represent the best interests of all student-athletes at all member institutions.

There are hints of progress in this area. The increased dialogue alone is a positive step, and in July of 1990 an NCAA subcommittee submitted recommendations for a "revolutionary" revenue-sharing plan. This plan, instigated by the huge CBS deal, would result in the average Division I school receiving a 90 percent increase in basketball tournament income, regardless of its success in postseason play. Still, the reforms must be adopted by the organization members, and the negative outcry came quickly. One critic of the plan was University of Nevada at Las Vegas athletic director Brad Rothermel. Said Rothermel, "Quite honestly, we pay the price to be there. We commit to basketball. We commit the money to be successful. The advantage in participating in the tournament has been that the more you went to it, the better your potential to generate revenue in the tournament. That will no longer be the case."[15] We can only hope that the last sentence of Rothermel's statement will turn out to be true.

Reform Coaching

The NCAA policy of financially rewarding successful member institutions is mostly responsible for that island of insanity known as Division I coaching. To secure the big chunks of revenue available through the NCAA's hypocritical method of revenue distribution, universities pay outrageous sums to procure the services of talented coaches. The University of Kentucky basketball coaching job, for instance, is reported to be worth $1 million per year. A million dollars a year to coach an amateur team of 18- to 22-year-olds whose primary purpose, according to university administrators and the credos of the NCAA, is to acquire an education. Certainly the pressure of a high-profile program like Kentucky's is intense, but just as certainly, this is all symptomatic of an idea run amok. No wonder some coaches ignore fairness and academics. Most people *would* do almost anything to keep a job worth hundreds of thousands of dollars per year, especially when institutions repeatedly hire and fire solely on the basis of winning percentage. Somewhere, somehow, the situation must be brought back into line. Although a successful coach may be perceived as "worth" more than an academic person at an institution, ideally the coach should not earn more than a university president or the dean of a professional college. The very notion communicates to student-athletes a secondary status for academics. Unfortunately, until the distribution of revenue is made more fair, little can be done to bring the head coaching position back down to earth. If progress is made in the area of revenue distribution, however, I would urge Division I institutions to reconsider the role of the college coach. Ideally, coaches should be part of the teaching faculty, be paid commensurately, and, like other professors, be eligible for tenure so that one lousy season would not result in a coach's getting the axe.

One area that could and should receive immediate attention in the college coaching profession is ethics. Restoring ethical behavior to the coaching ranks should be a primary goal of the National Association of Basketball Coaches (NABC) and the American Football Coaches Association (AFCA), the two professional organizations to which most coaches belong. A head coach *does* control his program, and he determines the ethical course that the program takes. Often heard are excuses for recruiting scandals and academic frauds, where a seemingly beleaguered head coach blames external factors over which he apparently had no control. This is pure baloney. If a head coach wants certain boosters to stay away from his players, he can control that. If a head coach wants his players to attend class, he can basically control that, too. The head coach holds the ultimate trump cards for his players: playing time and team membership. To pretend that he lacks the power and ability to control his own realm is poor acting fraught with lame excuses.

All head coaches know that they determine the character of their own programs. But disciplining a key player by taking the ball out of his hands might result in the loss of a key game, which might result in the eventual loss of a lucrative contract. This is the dilemma facing many coaches. Run a program in an ideal ethical manner with the proper balance between athletics and academics, and you may be operating with a handicap because other coaches are definitely not doing likewise. Here is where the coaching profession must step in. Instead of seeing and hearing and speaking no evil, coaches should establish an honor system in which cheaters and scoundrels are ousted from the profession. The attitude that "I won't tell on this person because I don't want anyone telling on me" only escalates abuses and encourages improprieties. The coaching profession must come to grips with this problem, and coaches collectively must develop methods of policing themselves to protect the integrity of their sports and the well-being of their student-athletes. I do not believe it is unreasonable to expect coaches, as do players in tennis, to "call their own lines." If they cannot, they should be briskly ushered out of the profession.

Dispel the Pro Myth

The 1989 Southwest Missouri State University basketball team featured six seniors, including five blacks and one white. One player graduated at spring commencement in May, two others graduated at the end of the summer session, one more was slated to graduate the following December, and a fifth hoped to receive his degree at the end of his fifth year. The final senior withdrew from school in the spring so that he could attend three NBA all-star tryout camps, where he was given a legitimate chance at making it in the professional ranks. This was all fine and dandy: Graduating five out of six seniors would have been an excellent accomplishment for the individual student-athletes and the program. But problems began to arise, problems that appeared to pose very serious threats to the academic plans of the two black seniors scheduled to receive degrees at future dates. Both players began to claim that they too were working toward professional basketball careers, and as the summer of 1989 wore on, their interest in academics began to wane as letters from various "scouts" and "agents" turned up in the players' mailboxes.

The notion of professional basketball careers for these players was ridiculous. Neither had the talent for even a low-level European league. In fact, they were extremely fortunate to have played Division I basketball. There was no reasoning with them, however. Here is an example of some dialogue between one of these players and me:

> **Academic Adviser:** (   ), you really need to get back on track. This NBA stuff is nonsense. You only shot 38 percent from the field in college, and you are 5'10". Get serious.
>
> **Player:** It was the system [style of play] that held me back. I never had the light—always giving up the rock. NOBODY has seen what I can really do.

These conversations went on for an entire summer, but sadly, they were to no avail. Fortunately, both players are still working toward their degrees, but they still hope eventually to play for money.

Dreams, acculturation, and fear of giving up the lifelong habit of playing ball are all responsible for many black players' unrealistic expectations regarding their chances in professional football and basketball. But other factors play a role, too, and one of these factors is the conduct of the agents and talent scouts who prey on the fantasies of eager young men. These leeches send random letters to players offering their "legal" services, or they hold "tryout" camps where kids pay their own money (often hundreds of dollars) to perform for a group of so-called professional scouts. These forms of lowballing are common in the world of Division I afterlife, and they only perpetuate the damaging pro myth. However, as despicable as some agents and scouts may be, they are not responsible for the pro myth situation. They only owe their parasitical existence to it.

The pro myth, as previously discussed, begins very early for many black youngsters and their families. Unfortunately, college coaches and their recruiting methods strengthen the stranglehold that the professional dream has on many black student-athletes. Selling a prospective player on the professional opportunities that await him if he attends a certain school is one of the most common recruiting ploys in the business. This is a major reason why the North Carolinas, Indianas, and Louisvilles always sign the cream of the freshman crop. Georgetown's John Thompson may have a deflated ball in his office to symbolize shattered pro dreams and the importance of academics, but he can afford that luxury because any high school senior considering Georgetown knows that his abilities will receive maximum national television exposure. He is all too aware of Patrick Ewing and the other fine players whom the Hoya program has catapulted into the professional ranks. Other coaches and programs are not so fortunate, and that is why Indiana State hard sells Larry Bird, Eastern Illinois proudly points to Kevin Duckworth, and Tulsa University coaches surely mention the example of Paul Pressey.

The problem with selling the pro opportunity in recruiting surfaces down the road. After a coach has convinced a kid to come to his program with the pro dream in mind, it becomes very difficult for the coach to turn around and say, "Okay, you have nary a chance at turning pro, and therefore, you had better concentrate on academics." Such chameleonic behavior would not be easy to carry out. First, it is hard to tell any young person to give up a dream, and second, coaches do not want the word getting around that they do doubt their players have a shot at the pros. Also, suppose one particular coach decides, in recruiting a prospective player, to deemphasize the professional aspect and concentrate solely on academic opportunities: This will put the coach and his program at a distinct disadvantage while competitors continue to stress pro possibilities. This is not meant to defend such action on the part of coaches—it is indefensible—but merely to explain why the scenario occurs again and again.

The only solution is for the NCAA and all coaches to deal unilaterally with the professional prospects for young players in a more open and honest manner. This could be accomplished if the coaching organizations adopted, as part of a code of ethics or honor system, a philosophy of not misleading prospective players on their pro potential to the point where academics become a secondary motivation. Also, the NCAA should make a concerted public relations effort within the sports themselves to educate players and coaches on any student-athlete's slim chances of playing his sport professionally. To help accomplish this, the NCAA could require all NCAA athletes to sign disclaimers, described earlier, that detail the importance of academics and the improbability of ever making it to the pros.

Hold Student-Athletes More Accountable for Their Actions

A significant contributor to the academic problems of student-athletes is the athletes' failure to accept responsibility for their scholastic endeavors. This should come as no surprise because these young men are rarely held accountable for any of their off-the-court actions. Parking fines often mysteriously disappear, huge long-distance phone bills are rung up on athletic department WATS lines, and recruiting transgressions involving illegal payments see institutions penalized while the implicated student-athletes get off scot-free and merely transfer to other schools. It is little wonder that many players assume academic obligations will be taken care of for them.

An excellent way to correct this irresponsibility would be to fairly hold student-athletes accountable for their misdeeds. No, a 17- or 18-year-old youngster should not be banished from sport for life for accepting an illegal recruiting inducement. But if improprieties have occurred, the student-athlete should share the blame for his role—perhaps a season's suspension for participating in recruiting or academic fraud. This would not only deter student-athletes from wrongdoing, it would deter coaches and programs as well. It would discourage the attitude of one well-known college basketball coach who reportedly told his assistants that he wanted to go to a Final Four and did not care what it took to get him there. If that coach had known that he would eventually lose the services of the players whom he cheated on, he might have been more cautious.

Make Freshmen Ineligible for Varsity Play

The only reasons for freshmen's playing varsity are financial ones that benefit the institutions. There is no logical argument against a 1-year transition period in which a freshman could play an abbreviated junior varsity schedule, acclimate himself to college life, and concentrate hard on his studies to get off to a successful start. A freshman ineligibility rule would also relieve some of the intense pressure of recruiting that comes from the "we have to have this kid next year" syndrome. It would simply slow the whole process down and bring sanity to the entire situation. Another positive effect of a freshman ineligibility rule would be to render moot the illogical and unfair Proposition 48 legislation.

Drop Proposition 48

If the freshman eligibility situation remains unchanged, the notorious Proposition 48 should be rescinded. There is little or no quantitative evidence that ACT and SAT scores are reliable and valid predictors of college success. High school grade point averages and core curriculum requirements are more reasonable and just, and the grade point average has been found to be a better predictor of academic success, anyway.

Institutions, within reason, should have the primary say in who is eligible to represent a school athletically. If a high school senior is qualified to attend a given institution, and his academic background (core curriculum classes and the minimum 2.0 grade point average) is such that he will not be obviously exploited, he should be allowed to compete and receive an athletic scholarship. If Harvard prefers not to play Lost Highway State University, so be it; they do not have to. Schools and conferences can choose to schedule games and associate with schools of their own ilk. At least with this type of system, no one could ever accuse the NCAA of denying opportunities to worthy young men who otherwise might not have them.

Learn Versus Earn

First, I strongly believe that academic support programs should be available to *all* college students. However, the issue at hand is academic support for the student-athlete, and this is what I will address.

Academic support programs should be moved from the athletic departments to the academic sides of the campuses. This would help prevent the serving-of-two-masters quandary and would alleviate the current tensions and suspicions between some faculty members and some athletic academic advisers. Additionally, academic advisers should encourage and help student-athletes to develop self-reliance instead of constantly hiring tutors. This hand-holding approach to academic support can be counterproductive by encouraging the abdication of responsibility. Academic support personnel *must* facilitate the development of self-respect, goal setting, and accountability for one's own actions. Only then will progress be made in solving the dilemmas facing so many academic advisers and Ballplayer Xs.

Some critics have suggested that Division I athletes in basketball and football should be paid, that this would end the hypocrisy and exploitation inherent in big-time intercollegiate sports. They see big-time college athletics as an entertainment industry and maintain that student-athletes, as the labor force, deserve a larger piece of the pie. Rick Telander, in his book *The Hundred Yard Lie*, advocates an Age Group

Professional Football League. Telander's league (the AGPFL) would essentially be a minor league with the top schools from the major conferences constituting the membership.[16] John Rooney's book, *The Recruiting Game*, promotes the same idea. Rooney suggests a "super-league" where players are drafted in a draft that is "organized along regional lines."[17] (Rooney is a geographer by trade.)

I have some real problems with the notion of "paying" student-athletes. First, where would the payments end? Fans and boosters pay money for the entire spectacle. Should the cheerleaders receive part of the revenue? The band? The student spectators themselves? They are definitely part of the television show. Maybe the three major networks should just issue a $10 check to everyone who walks into a stadium or arena. Obviously, the athletic competition is the primary event, but a host of other people are involved in many different ways. Second, it seems to me that the student-athletes are already getting paid. Thousands of dollars in tuition, books, and room and board represent a tidy little wage. For example, at Southwest Missouri State (a relatively inexpensive school to attend), an athletic scholarship is worth around $10,000. Throw in another $1,700 in Pell Grant money (the maximum allowed by the NCAA for students who qualify), plus summer jobs that are almost always found and provided, and you have quite an annual sum. Now take into account that student-athletes *should* be pursuing a college degree that will hopefully turn into a lifetime of earnings, and you can see that Division I participants have much to gain as it is.

The problem, as I see it, is not the fact that student-athletes fail to reap a percentage of the profits. It is rather the prevailing insanity that makes Americans and their corporations throw millions of dollars into sports/ entertainment rather than investing in the academic pursuits of our nation's schools. The denigration of academics is the issue, and I cannot fathom how paying players a small extra amount of cash is going to help that. Certainly, if student-athletes are making money for a university and the greenbacks are doing nothing more than lining the pockets of a successful coach, something is drastically wrong. That is why I would like to see institutions put profits back into the academic pursuits of the athletes themselves, the reason they should be there in the first place.

If NCAA member schools cannot devise a way to apply revenues to the academic interests of the participants and their scholastic programs, then somebody (university presidents, Congress, anyone with a conscience) should step in and end the current hypocrisy by demanding that the NFL and NBA develop and fund adequate minor-league systems, separate from the structure of intercollegiate competition.

Establish Degree Programs in Athletics

Thespians major in theater, dancers major in dance, and musicians major in music. Why not let athletes major in athletics? An athletic major would allow some student-athletes to take courses in subjects that interest them, and it would effect an end to general studies degree programs and other academic shenanigans. Of course, as in any other major, general education courses would be mandatory. The athletic major would also come under the same jurisdiction as any other degree program offered by an institution.

Athletic degree programs could be modeled somewhat on the European notion of the sports college. A graduate with a degree in athletics could consider coaching or directing a youth program as a viable career opportunity. Because sports are obviously important and big business in the United States, why not admit this and legitimize athletics as an academic pursuit?

The Opportunity

It is often said that where there is a challenge, there is also an opportunity. This appears to be the situation for the NCAA and big-time intercollegiate athletes. A strong challenge certainly exists, especially to provide appropriate academic programs for minority student-athletes. The NCAA and its member institutions are not unique in having to deal with some harsh realities. In fact, their problems only mirror the tough questions facing Americans and their society. Consider the following educational and demographic forecasts:

- The future will find more children entering school from impoverished backgrounds.
- More children will be entering school from single-parent households.
- The national demographic picture will feature more children from minority backgrounds, and the populations of the nation's public schools will obviously reflect this trend.
- A higher percentage of children will be born to teenage mothers.
- There will be a larger number of children who were born prematurely, leading to a higher incidence of learning difficulties among school children.
- There will be more children whose parents were not married.
- There will be a continuing high dropout rate among Hispanics, of whom only about 40 percent currently graduate from high school.
- There will be a continuing decline in the number of minority high school graduates who apply for college.[18]

This is a bleak portrait indeed, especially if one believes that many of the academic difficulties of student-athletes are directly related to inadequate educational opportunities, which in turn result directly from disadvantaged economic backgrounds. And, unfortunately, there is no reason to believe that an economic upswing is going to suddenly take place and reverse the trends currently restricting educational opportunities for the nation's poor and minorities. Black representation in the skilled occupations, for example, is already low, and there are no predictions that it will improve significantly in the near future. Blacks, who make up approximately 12 percent of the United States citizenry, only hold about 4 percent of the nation's managerial positions, 4.3 percent of the professional positions, and 7 percent of the government executive jobs.[19] These figures may remain stagnant, also; a U.S. Department of Labor report entitled *Workforce 2000* bluntly states, "Black men and Hispanics face the greatest difficulties in the emerging job market."[20]

Why is this? How can minorities, blacks in particular, having realized some meager yet positive gains in employment opportunities over the last 20 years, suddenly be facing a new series of economic challenges? An economy in transition and an evolving demographic picture are the primary reasons. To put it simply, future jobs will require more skills and stronger academic backgrounds. Although blacks and other minorities will constitute a larger share of the workforce (something that appears deceptively positive at face value), their heavy concentration in the declining central cities places them in locales where rich educational experiences are extremely difficult to obtain. A 1986 National Alliance of Business document clearly details this problem:

> The most rapidly growing yet most vulnerable of the nation's labor pool is concentrated where schools are inferior, work experience opportunities are poorest, and available full-time jobs are declining. Although business will need these workers, they will not be prepared to work and will too often find jobs inaccessible to transportation.[21]

Technological advancements and the nature of the economy are responsible for this situation, as the very characteristics of employment and careers are changing daily. Instead of a preponderance of tedious factory jobs, the year 2000 will see service jobs making up nearly 90 percent of all positions involved with "generating, processing, retrieving, or distributing information" via a system that will be heavily computerized.[22] Unfortunately, if current demographic trends continue until the end of the century, some pessimistic futurists see an American literacy rate of only 30 percent.[23]

Although the economic outlook for minorities in the United States is bleak, there is a glimmer of hope. Because of the lowered birth rates of the white majority during the last 3 decades, the nation is "entering an era in which youth will be in short supply."[24] Admittedly, a higher percentage of these youths will be poor, members of minority groups, and living in decaying urban areas, but there is a silver lining to this. For the first time, there will be more jobs available than there are *qualified* workers to fill them. "Qualified" is the key word here, because if the poor urban minorities are to seize the employment chances that this situation presents, they must work for and receive vastly improved schooling. The new, more technical employment will require workers to participate in ongoing technical training programs, trade seminars, workshops, and formal training at local technical institutes and colleges. Obviously, successful involvement in this new work force mandates literacy and adequate mastery of other basic skils.

The pertinence of the situation is the opportunity it presents for the NCAA and the athletic departments of its member institutions. If all of the involved parties could step back, momentarily forget about gate revenues and television rights, and thoughtfully examine the big picture, they might stumble onto the potential for positive action that is before them. At a time when the United States economy is at a crucial juncture, when skilled minority workers *must* become a viable part of the work force, when the educational prospects for minority youths may appear dismal, and when intercollegiate athletics and its academic handling of these same minority youths has come under attack and scrutiny, it is apparent that NCAA Division I athletics has the chance to become a leader in something that transcends bowl games and Final Fours.

Through its reliance on and the ensuing popularity of black student-athletes, the NCAA can be highly instrumental in developing the academic role models so sorely needed by the black community. But this means more than a 30-second public service announcement on television; it requires a concerted effort by university administrators, athletic directors, coaches, players, and the NCAA itself. Further, a few exclusionary rules (such as Proposition 48) do not constitute a legitimate or satisfactory effort on the part of the organization and its members. *Opportunity* must be the byword. If one poor student-athlete who otherwise could not have attended college can graduate, return to his community, and help 10 other disadvantaged youths improve themselves, then success has been achieved. This must become the mission, and not victories, revenues, titles, nor championships. The NCAA, like many youthful beings, has a little growing up to do.

To clarify their goals and define their mission, coaches and administrators should keep a few salient facts in mind:

- When a conference championship becomes the all-consuming goal, remember that youth unemployment rates are currently triple the overall unemployment rate.
- When an NCAA tourney selection committee makes what may seem an ill-advised decision, remember that 25 percent of all young black males have never held a job.
- When a prominent booster's demand for better seating seems too much, remember that one out of every four ninth-graders, over 1

million kids, will drop out of high school each year. In some cities, 50 percent will drop out before graduation.

- The next time a ballyhooed recruit turns elsewhere for a collegiate career, remember that one child in five lives in poverty.
- The next time it seems that winning a key game is the only thing that matters, remember the words of former Secretary of Labor William Brock:

> Millions of young workers are prevented from getting jobs or moving to better jobs because of their lack of basic competency in reading, writing and speaking English, by their poor math skills and by their lack of reasoning and problem solving skills.[25]

In other words, the proper priorities must be kept in focus; the future of the nation and *all* of its children may depend on it.

There will always be those who claim that allowing less-than-stellar students to participate in intercollegiate athletics "perverts" the university mission. They see the university as an ideal place, reserved for the academic elite and their scholarly pursuits. But the world is not an ideal place, and somebody has to accept the responsibility for giving opportunities to those who would be denied them otherwise. The NCAA and its various athletic activities is as good a starting place as any.

There is another aspect to the issue of "perverting the university mission," also. Gary R. Roberts, professor of law at Tulane University, states:

> This academic mission is not perverse or inherently inconsistent with a primary scholarly mission. Universities have always admitted students who do not meet normal academic criteria because they possess unique nonacademic talent—e.g., artists, musicians, and actors. Such students come primarily to develop skills, not their intellect, but the university's mission is not perverted or undermined. It reflects clear racial and class prejudice to endorse training artists, musicians, and actors who engage in traditionally white gentile endeavors, but then to argue against training sweaty, often minority athletes whose fans include beer-drinking blue collar people is perverse.[26]

Certainly, few people advocate the mere "training" of student-athletes, but Roberts's point on the latent racism involved in much of the criticism of Division I athletics is worth considering.

In chapter 6, the story of University of Arkansas player Dean Tolson was used to illustrate the academic shams that have often occurred in high school and intercollegiate athletics. But there is an opposite side to this story. Tolson, who eventually earned his degree at age 36, would possibly have dropped out of high school and never made it to college at all without his participation and skill in basketball. Is the Tolson story a tragedy or a success? Yes, academic fraud was committed, but Tolson did get his degree. Perhaps his example will prevent others from taking the same unfortunate early course.

These are the questions that must be considered, and everyone must hope for and work toward the day when the NCAA and its Division I institutions can get it right the first time around for youngsters and a nation that can surely benefit from it.

Notes

Chapter 2   The Dumb Jock: Fact or Fiction?

1. Jerome Cramer, "Winning or Learning? Athletics and Academics in America," *Phi Delta Kappan*, May 1986, K-1.
2. Ibid., K-2.
3. Alvin P. Sanoff and Kathryn Johnson, "College Sports' Real Scandal," *U.S. News and World Report*, 15 September 1986, 63.
4. Michael R. Steele, *Knute Rockne, A Bio-Bibliography* (Westport, CT: Greenwood Press, 1983), 34.
5. Ibid., 34.
6. Ibid., 20.
7. Robert J. Ballantine, "What Research Says: About the Correlation Between Athletic Participation and Academic Achievement," ED233994, 1981, 2.
8. Harry Edwards, "The Black Dumb Jock," *The College Board Review*, Spring 1984, 8.
9. Leroy Ervin, Sue A. Saunders, and H. Lee Gillis, "The Right Direction but Short of the Mark," *The College Board Review*, Spring 1984, 16.
10. Comptroller General of the U.S. "Review of Two Studies of College Graduation Rates," Washington, DC, Rept. GAO-B-220175, 10 September 1985, 5–6.
11. Ibid., 7–8.
12. Ervin, 17.
13. Ballantine, 4.
14. Ibid., 4.
15. Ann M. Mayo, "Athletes and Academic Performance: A Study of Athletes at an NCAA Division I Institution," *Academic Athletic Journal*, Fall 1986, 25–33.
16. Ibid., 27.
17. Ibid., 30.
18. Timothy L. Walter et al., "Predicting the Academic Success of College Athletes," *Research Quarterly for Exercise and Sport* 58, no. 2 (1987): 275.
19. "Commission's Study of Student-Athletes Released," *The NCAA News*, 5 December 1988, 15.

20. "Research Institute Releases Study of Black Student-Athletes," *The NCAA News*, 5 April 1989, 1.
21. James Marcotte, *Comparison of Academic Success Between CTC Basketball Players and Nonplayers* (Cincinnati, OH: Cincinnati Technical College, Office of Developmental Education, 1986), 1.
22. Sanoff, 62.
23. *NCAA Manual* (Mission, KS: The National Collegiate Athletic Association, 1989-1990), 316.
24. Sanoff, 62.
25. Comptroller General of the U.S., 5.
26. Chris Landis, "Bill May Expose Colleges That Exploit Athletes," *U. The National College Newspaper*, October 1988, 1, 22.
27. Ervin, 16.
28. "1988 Division I Academic Reporting Compilation," *The NCAA News*, 13 June 1990, 12.
29. Ervin, 17.
30. Walter, 277.
31. "Race Becomes the Game," *Newsweek*, 30 January 1989, 56.
32. Ballantine, 3.
33. J.E. Vader, ed., "Fast Breaks," *Women's Sports and Fitness*, October 1987, 45.
34. Cramer, K-3.

Chapter 3   The Roles and Educational Characteristics of the Student-Athlete

1. Walter Pauk, *How to Study in College* (Boston: Houghton Mifflin, 1989), 3–11.
2. Ibid., 19.
3. Rosemary Thompson, "Improving the Academic Performance of Athletes," *NASSP Bulletin*, October 1986, 15.
4. Donald F. Soltz, "Athletics and Academic Achievement: What is the Relationship?" *NASSP Bulletin*, October 1986, 22.
5. Janice Roberts Wilbur, Michael Wilbur, and Joseph R. Morris, "The Freshman Athlete's Transition: Athletic and Academic Stressors," *Academic Athletic Journal*, Spring 1987, 27.
6. "NCAA Forum," *The NCAA News*, 15 February 1989, 13.
7. Ibid., 16.
8. *Early Childhood Development Act* (Senate Bill 658), Missouri Department of Elementary and Secondary Education, January 1985, 9-10.
9. Robert L. Sinclair and Ward J. Ghory, *Reaching Marginal Students: A Primary Concern for School Renewal* (Berkeley, CA: McCutchan, 1987), 18.
10. *The Technology of Prevention* (Tucson, AZ: Associates for Youth Development, Inc., 1986), 4.

11. Tim O'Connor, "Widespread Problem Takes Toll on Students' Lives and Society," *Kansas City Times*, 23 May 1988, A-6.
12. *The Technology of Prevention*, 4.
13. *Employment Policies: Looking to the Year 2000* (Washington, DC: National Alliance of Business, 1986), i–ii.
14. Sinclair, 61–85.
15. Ibid., 14.
16. *The Technology of Prevention*, 4.
17. "Missouri Facts . . .," (Springfield, MO: Job Council of the Ozarks, 1986), 10.
18. Sinclair, ix–xvi.
19. Harold L. Hodgkinson, *All One System: Demographics of Education—Kindergarten Through Graduate School* (Washington, DC: The Institute for Educational Leadership, Inc., 1985), 9.
20. Ibid., 5.
21. Ibid., 5.
22. Ibid., 5.
23. Karen D'Angelo Bromley, *Language Arts: Exploring Connections* (Boston: Allyn & Bacon, 1988), 18.
24. Dorothy Grant Hennings, *Communication In Action: Teaching the Language Arts* (Boston: Houghton Mifflin, 1982), 295.
25. Mildred R. Donoghue, *The Child and the English Language Arts* (Dubuque, IA: Wm. C. Brown, 1985), 28.
26. Hennings, 413.
27. Ibid., 414.
28. Bromley, 18.
29. Hennings, 414.
30. Ibid., 414.
31. Ibid., 414.
32. Ibid., 414.
33. Clarence Underwood, Jr., "Advising of Black Student-Athletes: Twelve Recommendations," *NACADA Journal*, March 1986, 11.
34. Nancy Larrick, "Illiteracy Starts Too Soon," *Phi Delta Kappan*, November 1987, 184.
35. Ibid., 184.
36. *The Literacy Connection* (Springfield, MO: The Literacy Connection, 1987), 2.
37. Larrick, 184.
38. Ibid., 184.
39. Ibid., 187.
40. Ibid., 184.
41. John A. Garraty, *The American Nation* (New York: Harper & Row, 1975), 511.
42. Bromley, 349.
43. Gary D. Funk and Becky Haseltine, "The Writing Process: A Means

to Improving Writing Skills of the Student-Athlete," *Academic Athletic Journal*, Spring 1987, 40.

44. U.S. Congress, Congressional Budget Office, *Trends in Educational Achievement*. CBO Study (April 1986), Rept. 59-115-0-86-1, 74-78.

45. "Students From Most Minority Groups Improve Scores on College Admission Tests This Year; Average Stable," *The Chronicle of Higher Education*, 30 September 1987, 1.

46. David Owen, "The S.A.T. and Social Stratification," *Journal of Education* 168, no. 1 (1986): 89.

47. Ibid., 89.

48. Ibid., 82.

49. Marvin J. Cetron, "Class of 2000: The Good News and the Bad News," *The Futurist*, November-December 1988, 14.

50. "Few Students Are Whizzes on Computers, Study Says," *St. Louis Post-Dispatch*, 6 April 1988, A-12.

51. Cetron, 14.

52. John Allen Paulos, "So What If You're a Computer Illiterate," *TWA Ambassador*, May 1988, 14.

53. Louis Castenell, "The Mismeasurement of Low-Income Blacks: A Quagmire for Counselors" (Paper delivered at the annual meeting of The American Educational Research Association, Washington, DC, 20-24 April 1987), 9.

54. Reginald Wilson, "Black Education in the World Workforce: A Demographic Analysis" (Paper delivered at the annual meeting of the National Alliance of Black School Educators, Washington, DC, 21 November 1986), 1.

55. Harry Edwards, "The Black Dumb Jock," *The College Board Review*, Spring 1984, 8.

56. Ibid., 10.

57. Ibid., 10.

58. Ibid., 13.

59. Ibid., 13.

60. Wilson, 8.

61. Hodgkinson, 15.

62. Ibid., 16.

63. Wilson, 8.

64. Hodgkinson, 16.

65. Ibid., 19.

66. O'Connor, A-6.

67. U.S. Department of Labor. *Youth 2000: Challenge and Opportunity*. Prepared by the Hudson Institute. June 1986, 18.

68. Wilson, 23.

69. E. Matthew Shulz et al., "The Association of Dropout Rates with Student Attributes" (Paper delivered at the annual meeting of the American Educational Research Association, San Francisco, CA, 16-20 April 1986), 8.

70. O'Connor, A-6.
71. Ibid., A-6.
72. Shulz, 6.
73. Edwin Walker, "Providing Positive Role Models for Young Black Males," *Phi Delta Kappan*, June 1988, 773.

Chapter 4   The View From the Ivory Tower:
The Institution's Role in the Plight of the Student-Athlete

1. Michael R. Steele, *Knute Rockne, A Bio-Bibliography* (Westport, CT: Greenwood Press, 1983), 25.
2. Linda Greene, "The New NCAA Rules of the Game: Academic Integrity or Racism," *Saint Louis University Law Journal* 28, no. 1 (1984): 144.
3. "Association Shows Surplus Again," *The NCAA News*, 4 January 1989, 8.
4. Keith Dunnavant, "The Era of Blame is Over," *Sports Inc.*, 9 January 1989, 18.
5. Ibid., 21.
6. Ibid., 21.
7. Keith Dunnavant, "Crisis: The Mother of Invention," *Sports Inc.*, 9 January 1989, 26–28.
8. Jerome Cramer, "Winning or Learning? Athletics and Academics in America," *Phi Delta Kappan*, May 1986, K-1–K-8.
9. "1987-1988 Honor Roll of Donors," *Southwest Missourian*, Fall 1988, 38.
10. Rick Telander, *The Hundred Yard Lie* (New York: Simon & Schuster, 1989), 130.
11. "Sacred Heart Adds Football, Two Other Varsity Programs," *The NCAA News*, 21 March 1990, 2.
12. Cheryl M. Fields, "Poor Test Scores Ban Many Minority Students From Teacher Training," *The Chronicle of Higher Education*, 2 November 1988, 1.
13. Martha McMillan, "The Retention of Collegiate Athletes as Minority Students and Future Teachers: A Case Study," *Academic Athletic Journal*, Spring 1987, 18.
14. Gary D. Funk and Hal D. Funk, "Roadblocks to Implementing the Writing Process," *The Clearing House*, January 1989, 222.
15. Gary D. Funk and Becky Haseltine, "The Writing Process: A Means to Improving Writing Skills of the Student-Athlete," *Academic Athletic Journal*, Spring 1987, 40.
16. Eloise Salholz and Ginny Carroll, "Georgia: A Flag on the Play," *Newsweek*, 24 February 1986, 60.
17. William Nack, "This Case Was One for the Books," *Sports Illustrated*, 24 February 1986, 36.
18. Ibid., 36.

19. Ibid., 36.
20. Cramer, K-9.
21. Chuck Reece, "Jan Kemp," *Ms.*, January 1987, 46.
22. Harry Edwards, "The Black Dumb Jock," *The College Board Review*, Spring 1984, 9.
23. "Program of the 82nd Annual NCAA Convention" (Legislation prepared by William B. Hunt, assistant executive director, and Daniel T. Dutcher, legislative assistant, for the National Collegiate Athletic Association, Nashville, TN, January 1988), 20.
24. Reece, 89.
25. Juollie Carroll, "Freshman Retention and Attrition Factors at a Predominantly Black Urban Community College," *Journal of College Student Development*, January 1988, 58.
26. Janice Roberts Wilbur and Michael Wilbur, "The Academic Game," *Academic Athletic Journal*, Spring 1986, 33.
27. Thomas A. Luken, "Commercialization and Corruption," *USA Today*, July 1987, 66.
28. Edwards, 8.
29. Ibid., 9.
30. Rosemary Clark Kellenberger, "Strong Back/Strong Mind, Mutually Exclusive," *Academic Athletic Journal*, Spring 1986, 33.
31. Ibid., 39.
32. Luken, 66.
33. Ladell Anderson, "Starting Basketball After Christmas Makes Sense," *The NCAA News*, 28 December 1988, 4.
34. Charlie Vincent, "All in All, Recruiting Process Can Be Described as Immoral," *The NCAA News*, 22 February 1989, 3.
35. Charles S. Farrell, "Turning Academic Rejects Into Students Who Also Play Top Basketball," *The Chronicle of Higher Education*, 25 March 1987, 36.
36. "Houston Football Program Placed on Three Years' Probation," *The NCAA News*, 21 December 1988, 18–19.
37. "Oklahoma Football Program Goes on Three-Year Probation," *The NCAA News*, 21 December 1988, 19–20.

Chapter 5   Society: Where It All Begins

1. Charles S. Farrell, "NCAA Division II Votes Academic Rules Over Objections of Black Colleges," *The Chronicle of Higher Education*, 14 January 1987, 41.
2. "Race Becomes the Game," *Newsweek*, 30 January 1989, 57.
3. Rick Telander and Robert Sullivan, "You Reap What You Sow," *Sports Illustrated*, 24 February 1989, 21-31.
4. Ibid., 31.
5. Jerry Kirshenbaum, "An American Disgrace," *Sports Illustrated*, 27 February 1989, 16.

6. Telander, 23.
7. J.E. Vader, ed., "Fast Breaks," *Women's Sports and Fitness*, October 1987, 45.
8. Ibid., 45.
9. "The Final Four," *Sports Illustrated*, 16 March 1989, advertising supplement.
10. Ibid.
11. David Owen, "The S.A.T. and Social Stratification," *Journal of Education*, 168, no. 1 (1986): 86.
12. Ibid., 85.
13. Harry Edwards, "The Black Dumb Jock," *The College Board Review*, Spring 1984, 8.

Chapter 6   Solving the Problems, or Creating New Ones?

1. Linda Greene, "The New NCAA Rules of the Game: Academic Integrity or Racism," *Saint Louis University Law Journal* 28, no. 1 (1984), 103.
2. Ibid., 107.
3. Ibid., 109.
4. Ibid., 109–110.
5. Ibid., 113.
6. Leroy Ervin, Sue A. Saunders, and H. Lee Gillis, "The Right Direction but Short of the Mark," *The College Board Review*, Spring 1984, 16.
7. "Presidents Commission to Review Governance Process," *The NCAA News*, 8 February 1989, 1.
8. "Commission's Study of Student-Athletes Released," *The NCAA News*, 5 December 1988, 1.
9. Ibid., 1.
10. Ibid., 1.
11. "Research Institute Releases Study of Black Student-Athletes," *The NCAA News*, 5 April 1989, 1.
12. Greene, 111.
13. *NCAA Manual* (Mission, KS: The National Collegiate Athletic Association, 1989-1990), 110, 113.
14. Charles S. Farrell, "NCAA Division II Votes Academic Rules Over Objections of Black Colleges," *The Chronicle of Higher Education*, 14 January 1987, 41.
15. Santee Ruffin, "Minimum Academic Standards: Yes," *NASSP Bulletin*, October 1986, 6.
16. Jill Lieber, "Never Too Old to Learn," *Sports Illustrated*, 30 May 1988, 50.
17. Ibid., 52.
18. Gary R. Roberts, "Big-Time College Athletics: Academic Eligibility Rules Are Elitist," *USA Today*, July 1987, 68.

19. Charles S. Farrell, "About 400 Freshman Athletes in Big-Time Sports are Ineligible to Compete Under New Rules," *The Chronicle of Higher Education*, 10 September 1986, 1, 34.
20. "Partial-Qualifier Data Shows Little Change," *The NCAA News*, 15 March 1989, 1–2.
21. "Prop 48 Claims Heavy Toll Among Black Athletes," *Kansas City Star*, 31 March 1989, C-1.
22. Ibid., C-1.
23. David Owen, "The S.A.T. and Social Stratification," *Journal of Education*, 168, no. 1 (1986): 82.
24. Ibid., 82.
25. Rosemary Clark Kellenberger, "Proposition 48—College Admissions Tests: Friend or Foe?" *Academic Athletic Journal*, Fall 1986, 14.
26. Owen, 86.
27. Kellenberger, 18.
28. "Research Institute Releases Study of Black Student-Athletes," 1.
29. Kellenberger, 19.
30. Greene, 118.
31. Ervin, 16.
32. Timothy L. Walter et al., "Predicting the Academic Success of College Athletes," *Research Quarterly for Exercise and Sport* 58, no. 2 (1987): 278.
33. Ibid., 278.
34. "Race Becomes the Game," *Newsweek*, 30 January 1989, 58.
35. Bob Gretz, "Academic, Gambling Issues Await," *Kansas City Times*, 6 April 1989, F-1.
36. Harold L. Hodgkinson, *All One System: Demographics of Education—Kindergarten Through Graduate School* (Washington, DC: The Institute for Educational Leadership, Inc., 1985), 12.
37. Thomas Harper, "Minimum Academic Standards: No," *NASSP Bulletin*, October 1986, 1–4.
38. Ervin, 18.
39. "Program of the 82nd Annual NCAA Convention" (Legislation prepared by William B. Hunt, assistant executive director, and Daniel T. Dutcher, legislative assistant, for the National Collegiate Athletic Association, Nashville, TN, January 1988), 20.
40. "Select Committee Laid Base for Sports Reform Movement," *The NCAA News*, 24 January 1990, 1.
41. "Legislation on Graduation Rates Revived," *The NCAA News*, 22 March 1989, 1, 3.
42. Ibid., 1.
43. Ibid., 3.
44. Howard C. Kramer, "Faculty Advising: Help for Student-Athletes" *NACADA Journal*, March 1986, 7.
45. Kellenberger, 4.

46. Ibid., 5.
47. Ann M. Mayo, "The Role of a Code of Ethics in Athletic Academic Counseling," *Academic Athletic Journal*, Spring 1986, 28.
48. Ibid., 27.
49. Steven C. Ender, "Assisting High Academic Risk Athletes: Recommendations for the Academic Advisor," *NACADA Journal*, October 1983, 6.
50. Jerome Cramer, "Winning or Learning? Athletics and Academics in America," *Phi Delta Kappan*, May 1986, K-7.
51. Roger E. Jones, "The Athletic Study Hall: An Alternative to Establishing a Minimum GPA," *NASSP Bulletin*, October 1986, 27.
52. Ibid., 27.
53. Ibid., 27-31.
54. Rosemary Thompson, "Improving the Academic Performance of Athletes," *NASSP Bulletin*, October 1986, 18.
55. Ibid., 16.

Chapter 7   A Few Sensible Suggestions

1. Alvin P. Sanoff and Kathryn Johnson, "College Sports' Real Scandal," *U.S. News and World Report*, 15 September 1986, 63.
2. Thomas A. Luken, "Commercialization and Corruption," *USA Today*, July 1987, 67.
3. Steve Robinson, "Continuing Ed for Jocks: Colleges Should Pay Tuition Until Athletes Earn Degrees," *Sports Illustrated*, 6 June 1988, 120.
4. "Race Becomes the Game," *Newsweek*, 30 January 1989, 58.
5. Ibid., 58.
6. Jerry Kirshenbaum, "An American Disgrace," *Sports Illustrated*, 27 February 1989, 18.
7. "Race Becomes the Game," 57.
8. Harold L. Hodgkinson, *All One System: Demographics of Education—Kindergarten Through Graduate School* (Washington, DC: The Institute for Educational Leadership, Inc., 1985), 7.
9. Harry Edwards, "The Black Dumb Jock," *The College Board Review*, Spring 1984, 13-14.
10. Ibid., 9.
11. Ibid., 13.
12. Ibid., 13.
13. Reginald Wilson, "Black Education in the World Workforce: A Demographic Analysis" (Paper delivered at the annual meeting of the National Alliance of Black School Educators, Washington, DC, 21 November 1986), 20.
14. Diana Pollard McCauley, "Effects of Specific Factors on Blacks' Per-

sistence at a Predominantly White University," *Journal of College Student Development*, January 1988, 51.

15. "New TV Plan Would Cause Changes in NCAA Revenue Sharing," *The News-Leader* (Springfield, MO), 12 July 1990, 3C.

16. Rick Telander, *The Hundred Yard Lie* (New York: Simon & Schuster, 1989), 211-221.

17. John Rooney, *The Recruiting Game* (Lincoln, NE: University of Nebraska Press, 1987), 178-210.

18. Hodgkinson, 10.

19. Ibid., 6.

20. *Workforce 2000* (Kansas City, MO: U.S. Department of Labor, 1986), 23.

21. *Employment Policies: Looking to the Year 2000* (Washington, DC: National Alliance of Business, 1986), 1.

22. Marvin J. Cetron, "Class of 2000: The Good News and the Bad News," *The Futurist*, November-December 1988, 9.

23. Ibid., 9.

24. Hodgkinson, 18.

25. "A Critical Message for Every American Who Plans to Work or Do Business in the 21st Century," The National Alliance of Business, 1988, 5.

26. Gary R. Roberts, "Big-Time College Athletics: Academic Eligibility Rules Are Elitist," *USA Today*, July 1987, 70.

Bibliography

Anderson, Ladell. "Starting Basketball After Christmas Makes Sense." *The NCAA News,* 28 December 1988, 4.

"Association Shows Surplus Again." *The NCAA News,* 4 January 1989, 1.

Ballantine, Robert J. "What Research Says: About the Correlation Between Athletic Participation and Academic Achievement." Washington, DC: U.S. Department of Education, 1981.

Bayliss, V.A., and N.L. Walker. *Bayliss/Walker Scales: Holistic Writing Evaluation Grades 1–6.* Springfield, MO: Southwest Missouri State University, 1988.

Bromley, Karen D'Angelo. *Language Arts: Exploring Connections.* Boston: Allyn & Bacon, 1988.

Carroll, Juollie. "Freshman Retention and Attrition Factors at a Predominantly Black Urban Community College." *Journal of College Student Development,* January 1988, 52–59.

Castenell, Louis. "The Mismeasurement of Low-Income Blacks: A Quagmire for Counselors." Paper delivered at the annual meeting of The American Educational Research Association, Washington, DC, 20-24 April 1987.

Cetron, Marvin J. "Class of 2000: The Good News and the Bad News." *The Futurist,* November-December 1988, 9–15.

"Commission's Study of Student-Athletes Released." *The NCAA News,* 5 December 1988, 1, 16–19.

Comptroller General of the U.S. "Review of Two Studies of College Graduation Rates." Washington, DC, Rept. GAO-B-220175, 10 September 1985.

Cramer, Jerome. "Winning or Learning? Athletics and Academics in America." *Phi Delta Kappan,* May 1986, K-1–K-8.

"A Critical Message for Every American Who Plans to Work or Do Business in the 21st Century." An advertising supplement to the *New York Times Magazine* from the National Alliance of Business, 1988.

Donoghue, Mildred R. *The Child and the English Language Arts.* Dubuque, IA: Wm. C. Brown, 1985.

Dunnavant, Keith. "Crisis: The Mother of Invention." *Sports Inc.,* 9 January 1989, 26–28.

Dunnavant, Keith. "The Era of Blame is Over." *Sports Inc.,* 9 January 1989, 17–21.

Early Childhood Development Act (Senate Bill 658). Missouri Department of Elementary and Secondary Education, January 1985.

Edwards, Harry. "The Black Dumb Jock." *The College Board Review*, Spring 1984, 8–14.

Eisenbath, Mike. "Test of Your Life." *St. Louis Post-Dispatch*, 2 February 1989, D-1, D-3.

Employment Policies: Looking to the Year 2000. Washington DC: National Alliance of Business, 1986.

Ender, Steven C. "Assisting High Academic Risk Athletes: Recommendations for the Academic Advisor." *NACADA Journal*, October 1983, 1–10.

Ervin, Leroy, Sue A. Saunders, and H. Lee Gillis. "The Right Direction but Short of the Mark." *The College Board Review*, Spring 1984, 15–19.

Farrell, Charles S. "About 400 Freshmen Athletes in Big-Time Sports are Ineligible to Compete Under New Rules." *The Chronicle of Higher Education*, 10 September 1986, 1, 34.

Farrell, Charles S. "NCAA Division II Votes Academic Rules Over Objections of Black Colleges." *The Chronicle of Higher Education*, 14 January 1987, 41–42.

Farrell, Charles S. "Turning Academic Rejects Into Students Who Also Play Top Basketball." *The Chronicle of Higher Education*, 25 March 1987, 36–38.

"Few Students Are Whizzes on Computers, Study Says." *St. Louis Post-Dispatch*, 6 April 1988, A-12.

Fields, Cheryl M. "Poor Test Scores Ban Many Minority Students From Teacher Training." *The Chronicle of Higher Education*, 2 November 1988, 1, A-32.

"The Final Four." *Sports Illustrated*, 16 March 1989, advertising supplement.

"Freak Condition Halts NBA Career." *Kansas City Star*, 4 February 1990, Sports-1.

Funk, Gary D., and Hal D. Funk. "Roadblocks to Implementing the Writing Process." *The Clearing House*, January 1989, 222–224.

Funk, Gary D., and Becky Haseltine. "The Writing Process: A Means to Improving Writing Skills of the Student-Athlete." *Academic Athletic Journal*, Spring 1987, 35–40.

Garraty, John A. *The American Nation.* New York: Harper & Row, 1975.

Greene, Linda. "The New NCAA Rules of the Game: Academic Integrity or Racism." *Saint Louis University Law Journal* 28, no. 1 (1984): 101–151.

Gretz, Bob. "Academic, Gambling Issues Await." *Kansas City Times*, 6 April 1989, F-1.

Harper, Thomas. "Minimum Academic Standards: No." *NASSP Bulletin*, October 1986, 1–4.

Hennings, Dorothy Grant. *Communication in Action: Teaching the Language Arts*. Boston: Houghton Mifflin, 1982.

Hodgkinson, Harold L. *All One System: Demographics of Education—Kindergarten Through Graduate School*. Washington, DC: The Institute for Educational Leadership, Inc., 1985.

"Houston Football Program Placed on Three Years' Probation." *The NCAA News*, 21 December 1988, 18–19.

Jones, Roger E. "The Athletic Study Hall: An Alternative to Establishing a Minimum GPA." *NASSP Bulletin*, October 1986, 26–31.

Kellenberger, Rosemary Clark. "Proposition 48—College Admissions Tests: Friend or Foe?" *Academic Athletic Journal*, Fall 1986, 1–14.

Kellenberger, Rosemary Clark. "Strong Back/Strong Mind, Mutually Exclusive." *Academic Athletic Journal*, Spring 1986, 33–35.

Kirshenbaum, Jerry. "An American Disgrace." *Sports Illustrated*, 27 February 1989, 16–19.

Kramer, Howard C. "Faculty Advising: Help for Student-Athletes." *NACADA Journal*, March 1986, 3–11.

Landis, Chris. "Bill May Expose Colleges That Exploit Athletes." *U. The National College Newspaper*, October 1988, 1, 22.

Larrick, Nancy. "Illiteracy Starts Too Soon." *Phi Delta Kappan*, November 1987, 184–189.

"Legislation on Graduation Rates Revived." *The NCAA News*, 22 March 1989, 1, 3.

Lieber, Jill. "Never Too Old to Learn," *Sports Illustrated*, 30 May 1988, 49–54.

The Literacy Connection. Springfield, MO: The Literacy Connection, 1987.

Luken, Thomas A. "Commercialization and Corruption." *USA Today*, July 1987, 65–67.

Marcotte, James. "Comparison of Academic Success Between CTC Basketball Players and Nonplayers." Cincinnati, OH: Cincinnati Technical College, Office of Developmental Education, 1986.

Mayo, Ann M. "Athletes and Academic Performance: A Study of Athletes at an NCAA Division I Institution." *Academic Athletic Journal*, Fall 1986, 25–33.

Mayo, Ann M. "The Role of a Code of Ethics in Athletic Academic Counseling." *Academic Athletic Journal*, Spring 1986, 27–30.

McCauley, Diana Pollard. "Effects of Specific Factors on Blacks' Persistence at a Predominantly White University." *Journal of College Student Development*, January 1988, 48–51.

McMillan, Martha. "The Retention of Collegiate Athletes as Minority Students and Future Teachers: A Case Study." *Academic Athletic Journal*, Spring 1987, 15–21.

"Missouri Facts . . ." Springfield, MO: Job Council of the Ozarks, 1986.

Nack, William. "This Case Was One for the Books." *Sports Illustrated*, 24 February 1986, 35–42.

National Committee on Excellence in Education. *A Nation at Risk: The Imperative for Educational Reform*. Washington, DC: U.S. Department of Education, 1983.

"NCAA Forum." *The NCAA News*, 15 February 1989, 12–19.

NCAA Manual. Mission, KS: The National Collegiate Athletic Association, 1989-1990.

"New TV Plan Would Cause Changes in NCAA Revenue Sharing." *The News-Leader* (Springfield, MO), 12 July 1990, 3C.

"1988 Division I Academic Reporting Compilation." *The NCAA News*, 13 June 1990, 12.

"1987-1988 Honor Roll of Donors." *Southwest Missourian*, Fall 1988, 38.

Oberlander, Susan. "New Athletic Director at U. of District of Columbia Will Try to Rescue a Floundering Program." *The Chronicle of Higher Education*, 2 November 1988, A33, A34.

O'Connor, Tim. "Widespread Problem Takes Toll on Students' Lives and Society." *Kansas City Times*, 23 May 1988, A-1, A-6.

"Oklahoma Football Program Goes on Three-Year Probation." *The NCAA News*, 21 December 1988, 19-20.

Owen, David. "The S.A.T. and Social Stratification." *Journal of Education*, no. 1, 1986, 81–92.

"Partial-Qualifier Data Shows Little Change." *The NCAA News*, 15 March 1989, 1-2.

Pauk, Walter. *How to Study in College*. Boston: Houghton Mifflin, 1989.

Paulos, John Allen. "So What If You're a Computer Illiterate." *TWA Ambassador*, May 1988, 12, 14.

"Payout Estimated at $35.5 Million." *The NCAA News*, 28 March 1990, 1.

"Presidents Commission to Review Governance Process." *The NCAA News*, 8 February 1989, 1.

"Program of the 82nd Annual NCAA Convention." Legislation prepared by William B. Hunt, assistant executive director, and Daniel T. Dutcher, legislative assistant, for the National Collegiate Athletic Association, Nashville, TN, January 1988.

"Prop 48 Claims Heavy Toll Among Black Athletes." *Kansas City Star*, 31 March 1989, C-1, C-2.

"Race Becomes the Game." *Newsweek*, 30 January 1989, 56–69.

Reece, Chuck. "Jan Kemp." *Ms.*, January 1987, 44–46, 88–90.

"Research Institute Releases Study of Black Student-Athletes." *The NCAA News*, 5 April 1989, 1, 19.

Roberts, Gary R. "Big-Time College Athletics: Academic Eligibility Rules Are Elitist." *USA Today*, July 1987, 68-70.

Robinson, Steve. "Continuing Ed for Jocks: Colleges Should Pay Tuition Until Athletes Earn Degrees." *Sports Illustrated*, 6 June 1988, 120.

Rooney, John. *The Recruiting Game*. Lincoln, NE: University of Nebraska Press, 1987.

Ruffin, Santee. "Minimum Academic Standards: Yes." *NASSP Bulletin*, October 1986, 6–8.

"Sacred Heart Adds Football, Two Other Varsity Programs." *The NCAA News*, 21 March 1990, 2.

Salholz, Eloise, and Ginny Carroll. "Georgia: A Flag on the Play." *Newsweek*, 24 February 1986, 60.

Sanoff, Alvin P., and Kathryn Johnson. "College Sports' Real Scandal." *U.S. News and World Report*, 15 September 1986, 62–63.

"Select Committee Laid Base for Sports Reform Movement." *The NCAA News*, 24 January 1990, 1.

Sherrington, Kevin. "The Toughest Job . . ." *Dallas Morning News*, 29 June 1987, 1-B, 11-B.

Shulz, E. Matthew, et al. "The Association of Dropout Rates with Student Attributes." Paper delivered at the annual meeting of the American Educational Research Association, San Francisco, CA, 16–20 April 1986.

Sinclair, Robert L., and Ward J. Ghory. *Reaching Marginal Students: A Primary Concern for School Renewal*. Berkeley, CA: McCutchan, 1987.

Soltz, Donald F. "Athletics and Academic Achievement: What is the Relationship?" *NASSP Bulletin*, October 1986, 21–24.

Steele, Michael R. *Knute Rockne, A Bio-Bibliography*. Westport, CT: Greenwood Press, 1983.

"Students From Most Minority Groups Improve Scores on College Admission Tests This Year; Average Stable." *The Chronicle of Higher Education*, 30 September 1987, 1, 34.

The Technology of Prevention. Tucson, AZ: Associates for Youth Development, Inc., 1986.

Telander, Rick. *The Hundred Yard Lie*. New York: Simon & Schuster, 1989.

Telander, Rick, and Robert Sullivan. "You Reap What You Sow." *Sports Illustrated*, 24 February 1989, 20–31.

Thompson, Rosemary. "Improving the Academic Performance of Athletes." *NASSP Bulletin*, October 1986, 15–19.

Underwood, Clarence Jr. "Advising of Black Student-Athletes: Twelve Recommendations." *NACADA Journal*, March 1986, 19-22.

U.S. Congress, Congressional Budget Office. *Trends in Educational Achievement*. CBO Study (April 1986), Rept. 59-115-0-86-1.

U.S. Department of Labor. *Youth 2000: Challenge and Opportunity*. Prepared by the Hudson Institute. June 1986.

Vader, J.E., ed. "Fast Breaks." *Women's Sports and Fitness*, October 1987, 45.

Vincent, Charlie. "All in All, Recruiting Process Can Be Described as Immoral." *The NCAA News*, 22 February 1989, 3.

Walker, Edwin. "Providing Positive Role Models for Young Black Males." *Phi Delta Kappan*, June 1988, 772-774.

Walter, Timothy L., Donald E.P. Smith, George Hoey, Rowena Wilhelm, and Samuel D. Miller. ''Predicting the Academic Success of College Athletes.'' *Research Quarterly for Exercise and Sport* 58, no. 2 (1987): 273–279.

Wilbur, Janice Roberts, and Michael Wilbur. ''The Academic Game.'' *Academic Athletic Journal*, Spring 1986, 31–34.

Wilbur, Janice Roberts, Michael Wilbur, and Joseph R. Morris. ''The Freshman Athlete's Transition: Athletic and Academic Stressors.'' *Academic Athletic Journal*, Spring 1987, 23–31.

Wilson, Reginald. ''Black Education in the World Workforce: A Demographic Analysis.'' Paper delivered at the annual meeting of the National Alliance of Black School Educators, Washington, DC, 21 November 1986.

Workforce 2000. Kansas City, MO: U.S. Department of Labor, 1986.

Index